The Slackers
and Other Plays

STUDIES IN AUSTRIAN LITERATURE, CULTURE, AND THOUGHT

The Slackers
and Other Plays

Peter Turrini

Translated and with an Afterword by
Richard S. Dixon

Ariadne Press

Library of Congress Cataloging-in-Publication Data

Turrini, Peter.
    [Plays. Selections. English]
    The slackers and other plays / Peter Turrini ; translated and with an afterword by Richard S. Dixon.
        p.   cm.--(Studies in Austrian literature, culture, and thought. Translation series)
    Plays translated from the German.
    Contents: A crazy day -- Joseph and Mary -- A social engagement -- The slackers.
    ISBN 0-929497-48-1
    1. Turrini, Peter--Translations, English. I. Title. II Series.
PT2682.U7A24 1991
832'.914--dc20   91-29570
                                                  CIP

Cover: Art Director: George McGinnes; Designer: David Hubble

Copyright©1992
by Ariadne Press
270 Goins Court
Riverside, California

All rights reserved.
No part of this publication may be reproduced or transmitted in any form or by any means without formal permission.
Printed in the United States of America.
ISBN: 0-929497-48-1

Peter Turrini   Photo courtesy of Dr. Bernhard Slavicek

Contents

A Crazy Day 1

Joseph and Mary 55

A Social Engagement 83

The Slackers 131

Afterword 225

A Crazy Day

or

The World Turned Upside Down

*With the
Stipulation
That
I do not
Write
About:
Authority
Relocation
Politics
Morality
The upper class
VIPs
The opera
The theater
or
Influential people*

*I may
With the approval
of one
or two
Censors
Write
Anything
I
Wish*

—Beaumarchais.

ACT ONE

A box, a huge carton closed on all sides. Noises are heard from inside the box—softly at first, then increasingly louder; this is followed by cries and screams. Suddenly, the front of the carton falls open with a loud boom. The players in this comedy stand with puzzled faces staring out into the audience. Figaro whistles and, with a wave of the hand, sends the players off stage. Darkness disappears gradually from inside the box. Inside, the box has two side doors and a large entrance in the middle of the rear wall. The doors have been cut simply out of the side walls. In one corner of the box: a comfortable armchair. The other furniture to be used in the course of the play stands in a distant corner, covered by a tarpaulin.

Figaro kneels, rear-end to the audience. He is cleaning the floor.

FIGARO: Indeed, my lord is kind. From his own stock of sixty-seven beds, he has given me one bed for my own. But how on earth could that noble derrière get along on only sixty-six?
Figaro grabs his rear-end and suddenly pivots about.
But, you know, even when you figure the combined total number of asses—kitchenmaids, chambermaids, cellarmaids and the like—it's still a lot of beds. I guess it's like my lord always says . . . before he lets me have it with the whip . . . "only the aristocratic is infinite." Indeed, my lord is kind. He works for the improvement of his servants with his own two fists . . . er . . . two hands.
Figaro continues to scrub the floor.
Let's see . . . eleven divided into forty-seven . . .
Susanne crawls in from the background and sits down upon Figaro's back.

FIGARO: Oh, heavenly burden! That must be Susanne—my Bride, my Angel. The Goddess of Seville and its surrounding metropolitan area . . .

SUSANNE: . . . Who is seated upon a jackass.

FIGARO: Than I'm the happiest jackass around . . .

SUSANNE: At least of Seville and its surrounding metropolitan area.
FIGARO: Never before has a more delicate weight caressed the butt-end of this backbone. Never before have two such blushing cheeks pressed against two other blushing cheeks . . .
SUSANNE: Stop beating around the bush . . . What are doing on the floor? You're on your knees in this god-forsaken room mumbling arithmetic yourself.
FIGARO: First of all, this is no ordinary god-forsaken room, this is our god-forsaken room. Second of all, I'm not mumbling arithmetic to myself, I'm measuring the area of our bed. And third of all, I've got to be on my knees 'cause you're sitting on my back!
SUSANNE: (*jumps up*): Our room? Our bed?
FIGARO (*stands up, assumes a "hurt" expression*): Will you listen for a minute before you start running at the mouth! His Excellency, the Duke Almaviva, in all his worldly wisdom and mercy has bestowed upon us his seven-hundred-twenty-fourth room and that over there is his sixty-seventh bed, which he has also given us, to do with as we see fit . . . Well, what do you say to that?
SUSANNE: Well, I say . . . well!
FIGARO: Well?
SUSANNE: Well . . . Well!
FIGARO: Huh?
SUSANNE: No.
FIGARO: What do you mean, "No"?
SUSANNE: What do you mean, "huh"?
FIGARO: Well, because between yes and no there exists a broad area . . . grounds . . .
SUSANNE: And if I have grounds not to name those grounds?
FIGARO: That's all the more grounds to tell me your grounds. Well?
SUSANNE: No.
FIGARO: Susie . . . I'll convince the Duke to give us his two-hundred-forty-fourth carpet . . . how's that? And the rest of the furniture we can bring down from the attic in unnoticeable installments.
SUSANNE: Figgie, this room is filled just by your being here.

FIGARO: Then forget the furniture.
SUSANNE: And the room.
FIGARO: What do you have against this room, anyway? Even the master's most cramped quarters are noble galleries for servants' love. And besides, it's set exactly between the chambers of our dear lord and his dear mistress.
SUSANNE: That's just it.
FIGARO: That's just it—one more advantage of this blessed, sacred chamber. During the night, when our dear mistress rings for the maid on account of her awful stomach-ache, one step and you're there! And should our dear lord need some unnecessary trifle at the utmost speed—presto! I stand at his disposal. You see, this room is a "step saver"—a time-saver for both of us.
SUSANNE: For all three of us, you mean.
FIGARO: What do you mean by that?
SUSANNE: I mean, that presto—you're gone and presto—the Duke's here.
FIGARO: He'd have to send me far enough away.
SUSANNE: He'd send you far enough away.
FIGARO: And if he sent me far enough away! Holy Castilian easter egg! A wretched suspicion raises its ugly head within my breast.
SUSANNE: Still, it's not a bad room at all, you know.
FIGARO: It's beginning to look bad to me. Do you really think the Duke wants to make a monkey out of me? Me?
SUSANNE: I know what I think. Bacillus has already extended to me the kind invitations of his most noble lord and master.
FIGARO: Bacillus, that foreign creep, that bulbous bringer of bad news—and ducal sentiments . . . If I ever get my hands on him, I'll fix it so he won't even remember his nickname when I get finished with him.
SUSANNE: He is a true creep after the Duke's own heart.
FIGARO: Wasn't it the Duke himself who did away with that awful practice of first night "visitation" rights?
SUSANNE: Only to decree it again—starting with me.
FIGARO: Well, this decree will cost him plenty.
SUSANNE: He's already made the first installments: my clothes.
FIGARO: What a generous advance for the favors of *my* beloved! And I thought it was my well-earned reward for my loyal

services. Sometimes, I'm so dumb it hurts!
SUSANNE: Figaro poses and the Duke disposes . . .
FIGARO: Not much longer. The wisdom of the great is based on the falsehoods of the small. Kiss me, Muse of all scoundrels! My kingdom for a good idea! I could demand satisfaction, as you husband, but at the level of Baron whether . . . I could kill him in a jealous rage . . . but even that excuse only works for the rich and noble. I could have him arrested on account of indecent behavior—but unfortunately the price of justice is high: it begins at one hundred dollars.
SUSANNE: Good legal advice *is* expensive.
Bell sounds.
SUSANNE: That's the duchess. I've gotta go.
FIGARO: Don't go so fast, my little turtledove, kiss me first! Kissing improves the thought processes, say all the doctors.
SUSANNE: And what will my husband say tomorrow, if I kiss my fiancé today?
FIGARO: I permit it—just this once.
Susanne kisses him lightly.
SUSANNE: Just this once.
A louder bell sounds.
FIGARO: What a kiss! I can hear bells!
SUSANNE (*frightened*): The Duchess!
Exit Susanne; Figaro alone.
FIGARO: So, she's gone, my dear. And I won't have that Duke buzzing around her either! My heart forbids it! Now it dawns on me—He promotes and makes me his messenger and while I ride out loyally on my appointed rounds, he's in there riding my Susanne. While I'm out taking care of his family affairs, he taking care of mine! If only horniness and poverty went together, we might just keep it away from these rich folks. But, as it is, your passion for my Susanne will be the passion that does you in, my lord. Figaro, what's a servant to do—when he isn't allowed jealousy or honor or justice? It gets bad around here: intrigue and lies and excuse all trespasses until some future date. With the flames of his own passion I'll skin that Duke alive and with fiery bravado take his privilege for my own! That is what I'd call justice.
Bartholo, a somewhat shoddy, unkempt doctor, and Marcelline, a woman who has seen better years, appear on stage.

BARTHOLO (*to Figaro*): Judas Priest! Is this uneducated nincompoop here again!
FIGARO: Judas Priest! Is this educated nincompoop here again!
BARTHOLO: If you have nothing more intelligent to push through those rotten teeth of yours, sir, then . . .
FIGARO: I don't want to strain you, sir.
BARTHOLO: You do that by your being here, sir.
FIGARO: Ditto, sir.
BARTHOLO: Sir!
FIGARO (*imitating*): Sir!
MARCELLINE: Gentlemen! Your civility is overextending the bounds of propriety.
FIGARO: Madame, I shall be delighted to deliver this unbearable presence into your hands. Farewell, sir, and try to think of a wedding gift that's at least fairly expensive.
BARTHOLO: How about Wedgewood arsenic?
Exit Figaro.
BARTHOLO: Mother Mary, that guy is more obnoxious than an old beggar. An open sore on a noble nose is always preferable to a servant's awful mug. And what are the sick, pale, tender lips of a countess compared to the stinking mouth of some fleshy milkmaid? Peter Paul and pestilence, why should those people ever get sick? God knows even when they're healthy they're disgusting enough.
MARCELLINE: You are always thinking of your work, aren't you?
BARTHOLO: Work makes you free! My good lady. But, to the point: Why have you called me here—is someone sick?
MARCELLINE: The Duke.
BARTHOLO: The Duke?
MARCELLINE: A horrible disease. He has these attacks . . . whenever he sees a beautiful girl.
BARTHOLO: Blood-poisoning!
MARCELLINE: And it seems to grow worse with the coming of night . . .
BARTHOLO: Rising fever, eh?
MARCELLINE: He's up half the night.
BARTHOLO: Oh!! A clear case of spotted fever.
MARCELLINE: A clear case of unfaithfulness.
BARTHOLO: This disease is not recognized in persons of wealth and high social standing.

MARCELLINE: Well, then, off the record: the duke sneaks over into the maids' chambers every night.
BARTHOLO: Let us say: the duke inspects his property by the shadowless light of the moon . . . or moons.
MARCELLINE: And tomorrow he is going to "inspect" this place, too.
BARTHOLO: A dutiful duke . . . hard-working.
MARCELLINE: And Susanne's bed.
BARTHOLO: Excellent! Then Figaro will get something to think about, the Duke will get something to smile about and Susanne will get . . . well . . .
MARCELLINE: And what about me?
BARTHOLO: We all must bear our burdens with the honor our age demands.
MARCELLINE: I should slug you for a remark like that. You low-down smart-ass. Isn't the reason I'm alone because you left me? If you hadn't broken your promise . . .
BARTHOLO (*sings*): "Promises, Promises." Do you always have to bring that up? What do you want? . . . that someday we get to celebrate the hundredth anniversary of our fleeting love affair?
MARCELLINE: I need you help, Doctor.
BARTHOLO: If it's not against the law or against my code of honor, of course.
MARCELLINE: I am in love with a man . . .
BARTHOLO: This disease occurs quite often.
MARCELLINE: Figaro.
BARTHOLO: Now that's not seen so often. Why would a mature woman like you flee into the arms of a kid like that?
MARCELLINE: Exactly because I am a "mature woman . . ."
BARTHOLO: Then why don't you marry him?
MARCELLINE: Mainly because he's marrying Susanne today.
BARTHOLO: Then I wouldn't marry him.
MARCELLINE: Is that all you can say, your only advice, Doctor?
BARTHOLO: Good advice isn't cheap.
MARCELLINE (*sidles up to him*): My presence used to be worth something to you . . .
BARTHOLO: Let's just say, "inflation" . . .

Marcelline counts out gold coins into Bartholo's open hand. He leaves his hand open, as if expecting more.

MARCELLINE: That's a high inflation rate, sir. OK, so advise, you greedy toad.
BARTHOLO (*clinking the gold pieces together in his hand*): Patience, patience . . . a good plan takes time . . . inspiration . . . you love Figaro?
MARCELLINE: That's it.
BARTHOLO: Figaro loves Susanne?
MARCELLINE: So it seems.
BARTHOLO: Interesting
MARCELLINE: Thank you.
BARTHOLO: Attenzione . . . Figaro marries Susanne and the Duke laughs all the way to her bed.
MARCELLINE: And I cry all the way to my grave.
BARTHOLO: Attenzione . . . what's more important to women than any morality?
MARCELLINE: Her reputation.
BARTHOLO: Figaro will turn his back on her.
MARCELLINE: And his eyes on me! Doctor, you are a genius when it comes to being low-down.
BARTHOLO: One does what one can.
MARCELLINE: Take this kiss with my thanks.
Susanne appears.
SUSANNE (*clearing her throat*): Excuse me, I didn't want to disturb the old folks at home. It's so sweet to see the flicker of love even in the twilight of life.
MARCELLINE: Twenty and already a smart-ass.
SUSANNE: Seventy and still horny.
MARCELLINE (*with exaggerated friendliness*): How're things with the Duke?
SUSANNE: He's all right.
MARCELLINE: All right enough to pay this room a visit now and then, eh?
SUSANNE: It's his house, he paid for it.
MARCELLINE: And Susanne's bed.
BARTHOLO (*imitating Susanne*): It's his house . . .
MARCELLINE: . . . He can do what he wants in it.
SUSANNE: How tragic that he won't do it with you.
MARCELLINE: You . . . high-class whore!
SUSANNE: Tsk, tsk. No beauty and no manners either. You really do just have your wrinkles to keep you warm.

MARCELLINE: Bitch!
SUSANNE: You know, your face looks like an accordion when you talk.
MARCELLINE: Hold me back, Doctor, or else I may do something I'd regret later on.
SUSANNE: Yes, doctor, hold on to that old woman or else she might actually do something.
BARTHOLO: For God's sake, stop I say.
SUSANNE: For God's sake, get out I say.
BARTHOLO: Let's go Marcelline. Susie is anxious to make a monkey out of her dearly beloved Figaro.
Exit Marcelline and Bartholo.
SUSANNE (*calling after them*): Hell begins two floors down; keep going.
Susanne alone.
SUSANNE: Now that's a pair for you. Those two could make all of the Americas unhappy. Why are they bugging me of all people? Is the love of a poor servant girl a kind of pasture where any old cow can tramp around? What have I done to them? I love Figaro, that's all. Yes, that's all. I *am* a rich woman; the eyes of my lover reach into the treasure of my heart. His hands caressed it long ago.
Music; the following is spoken to musical accompaniment.
In the eyes of my songbird
Spain's twilight sleeps
Olives grow beneath wings
in thousand-year vases
Come, pretty songbird
Give me a blood-red Spain
Genoa and the world over,
And your songbird's heart
And your songbird's feathered heart . . .
Cherubin enters.
CHERUBIN: Susanne sings?
SUSANNE: Susanne laughs.
CHERUBIN: Cherubin weeps.
SUSANNE: That's not what a happy page is s'posed to do.
CHERUBIN: But for a fired page?
SUSANNE: Did some girl tell you to get lost?
CHERUBIN: Worse.

SUSANNE: Worse than that?
CHERUBIN: Much worse. My boss told me to get lost. Specifically, the Duke.
SUSANNE: What's that old goat got against a young thing like you?
CHERUBIN: This young thing seems to have hung around a certain Miss Blanchette a few too many times. You might say I wanted to tutor her in Basic Anatomy. Such a good student, too!
SUSANNE: And?
CHERUBIN: A bitter awakening! Suddenly the Duke comes running in and screams that the cows are out. He screams . . .
SUSANNE: What?
CHERUBIN: Just that.
SUSANNE: Namely . . .
CHERUBIN: Namely, that if I thought I was the biggest stud in Castille and that I could go around riding his housemaids I was mistaken and . . .
SUSANNE: That's enough.
CHERUBIN: Enough to get fired. Susie, help me or else I'll be banished from your sight forever!
SUSANNE: I'd feel awful.
CHERUBIN: I'd die.
SUSANNE: You'd survive.
CHERUBIN: A living corpse. Ragged and hungry, I'd make my way through the German swamps, my weary eyes searching in vain for the comfort of your beauty . . .
SUSANNE: Now, just a minute, fugitive from a chain-gang, isn't the Duchess your secret love? Or have you already gone through all the housemaids and now it's my turn?
CHERUBIN: You're right. But the Duchess is so far away that I can only talk about her. You, however, I can love.
SUSANNE: Thank God you're not so far away that I can't box your ears now and then.
She runs after him.
CHERUBIN: Save me, Susanne, or I'm lost!
Susanne laughs and stops chasing.
SUSANNE: How can I make the Duke change his mind?
CHERUBIN: Rumor has it he likes you.
SUSANNE: And rumor has it you're too smart for you own good.

CHERUBIN: Put in a good word for me.
SUSANNE: During the pauses, you mean?
CHERUBIN: Whenever.
SUSANNE: Why does everyone want to use me for his own purposes! My love is not for hire, it's mine!
CHERUBIN: I don't understand you, Susie.
SUSANNE: I don't understand you either, Cherubin.
Offstage: voices and steps approaching.
CHERUBIN: Susie, I hear something.
SUSANNE: Oh my God! The Duke!
CHERUBIN: The Duke! Oh my God!
Cherubin disappears quickly beneath an armchair. The Duke enters. Ahead of him a servant. The servant knocks three times on the floor with a cane. Everyone freezes in position.
SERVANT: His Excellency, the particularly high-born well-heeled Duke Almaviva, Lord of two hundred cattle and chambermaids, count of Castille and Catalonia, high judge for the Inquisition, chief stockholder in the Gallows holy orders of the Spanish Empire, Chairman of the Holy Spanish League for the Extermination of Heathens, Most honored Duke . . .
DUKE: That's enough. I'm s'posed to be here incognito. Susanne, I have come here in person to express my feelings toward you. I find myself in the unfortunate position of possessing a certain passion for you. I will proceed to make myself clear . . . May I sit down?
SUSANNE: Wait. my lord, with your permission, I'd prefer if you stood.
DUKE: With your permission, I would like to sit down.
SUSANNE: With your permission, the Duke seems to me particularly handsome when he stands.
DUKE: With your permission, the Duke seems to feel particularly comfortable when he sits.
Duke sits; Cherubin screams in pain.
DUKE: Who screamed?
SUSANNE: Screamed? Someone screamed?
Duke stands up, sits down—again Cherubin screams.
DUKE: Someone screamed!
SUSANNE: Squeaking . . . It's an old chair.
Duke stands up, sits down. Cherubin attempts to imitate the sound of a chair squeaking.

DUKE: Squeaking, you're right. Someone oughta get that fixed. Susanne—I love you. Bacillus has already informed you of my burning passion. I have come personally to speak with you about the logistics of the situation. Relax, my child.
SUSANNE (*with emphasis*): My lord, I intend to marry Figaro *today*.
DUKE: That's the first point in my plan. He'll be the father of course.
SUSANNE (*with renewed emphasis*): Figaro has always served you faithfully.
DUKE: That's the second point in my plan. His faithfulness will be rewarded. I'm promoting him to the Foreign Service and naming him my special courier.
SUSANNE (*begging*): Figaro has always served you well.
DUKE: And with his absence he will serve me in the best possible manner—since it will guarantee me your "undisciplined" presence. That's the third point in my plan.
SUSANNE (*playfully*): There's one more point.
DUKE: One more? I pay that Bacillus to think up the best intrigues possible. Did he leave something out?
SUSANNE: The most important one—I don't love you.
DUKE: That does change things. Bacillus! (*Louder.*) Bacillus! *Bacillus, shabbily dressed, crawls out from the tarpaulin which still covers the furniture.*
DUKE: Bacillus—she doesn't love me. I need a new intrigue. Get to work, genius.
BACILLUS: Let me think, let me think . . . Got it! She doesn't love you, yet she does love someone. Old women are all dried up, can't do anything with them—but her! She's still young and full of fire . . . a fire which your servant is going to quell. It's simple: get rid of the servant and quell the fire yourself. She's young and burning with passion.
SUSANNE: The Duke may scorch his fingers.
DUKE: A bad plan: it's already been tried. Think of another.
BACILLUS: Let me think . . . I've got it. Listen, what you can't steal you can buy, my lord. Love is an expensive thing for your servant to own. Give him twenty bucks and you've got her.
DUKE: How much do I owe you, Susanne?
SUSANNE: You want to buy my love? Well, then—the first pay-

ment is due now.
SUSANNE: Oh, not much, my lord. I hear you fired your page Cherubin today . . . hire him back.

DUKE: How much, my child?
SUSANNE: Oh, not much, my lord. I hear you fired your page Cherubin today . . . hire him back.
DUKE: Why is he so important to you?
SUSANNE: Why is it so important to you?
DUKE: The creep has fallen in love with Blanchette.
SUSANNE: Why is Blanchette so important to you?
DUKE: Bacillus, why is Blanchette so important to me?
BACILLUS: She has such a beautiful . . . mind.
DUKE: Yes. He was fired for stealing private property. I caught him at it myself. Tell him about it, Bacillus.
BACILLUS (*assumes a dramatic pose*): Our dearly beloved Duke Almaviva was on an inspection trip. Entering Blanchette's room he finds said room in complete disarray. The Duke becomes highly suspicious and lifts the bed-spread . . . peeks beneath . . .
Bacillus lifts the spread which has been draped over the armchair and suddenly he espies . . .
Bacillus sees Cherubin
. . . Oh!
SUSANNE: Oh!
BACILLUS: Cherubin!
DUKE: Under the bed!
BACILLUS: Under the chair!
DUKE (*jumps up*): Oh! (*He takes a look for himself.*) The guy lives under my furniture.
CHERUBIN: Coincidence, my lord.
SUSANNE: A mistake, my lord.
DUKE: A disgrace, Susanne.
BACILLUS: Reprehensible.
DUKE: Disgusting—so soon before the wedding and already lovers are lurking under the furniture. What immoral servants do I have! Disgusting—high crimes against the peace of this house. Poor Figaro, I love him like he was one of my own racehorses . . . and to think . . .
BACILLUS: Disgusting.
DUKE: Stop interrupting . . . what were we talking about anyway?
BACILLUS: You were just mentioning the sad fact of a screwed-over thoroughbred.

DUKE: Thoroughbred?
BACILLUS: Figaro.
DUKE: The poor deceived jackass.
SUSANNE: Not a thoroughbred or a jackass. My lord, Figaro is not deceived and Cherubin is . . .
CHERUBIN: An innocent victim of circumstance!
DUKE: Same as yesterday. The guy's an innocent victim.
SUSANNE: And it was because of "yesterday" that he came to me today. After you caught him with Blanchette, you fired him. Before you found him here, he was begging me to beg you not to fire him.
DUKE: Does he beg better underneath the armchair?
BACILLUS: Disgusting!
DUKE: Enough! This whorehouse atmosphere will have to change. (*Striking an "official" aristocratic stance*) I decree . . .
SERVANT (*pounding the floor three times with a cane*): Hear ye, hear ye, His Majesty the Duke of Almaviva, Lord of . . .
DUKE (*interrupting*): Shut up, will ya. This ceremonial stuff is starting to get on my nerves. (*To Susanne.*) I'm looking forward to informing Figaro of your disgusting behavior.
SUSANNE (*defiantly*): And I'm looking forward to informing the Duchess of your disgusting intentions. Tit for tat, if you'll excuse the expression.
DUKE: Jesus, Mary and Joseph . . . Why, that's . . .
BACILLUS: Disgusting.
DUKE: Blackmail!
BACILLUS: Reprehensible—the servants are becoming more and more unmanageable.
DUKE (*to Susanne*): You dare?!
SUSANNE: I dare.
DUKE: Bacillus, she dares not. Quick, a new intrigue.
    A knock at the door.
BACILLUS: Someone's at the door!
DUKE: Open it.
BACILLUS: Coming!
DUKE: Wait! First think up a new intrigue.
    A second knock, louder.
BACILLUS: They're still out there—I'd better open . . .
DUKE: Wait—a plan, we need a plan! Quick!
BACILLUS: A plan? Just like that? Why, I can't . . . Oh God . . .

The door opens: enter Figaro and the Duchess.
BACILLUS: Disgusting. I don't think I'm s'posed to be in this scene.
FIGARO (*to the Duke, with the politest of bows*): Oh, happy servants, my lord, who have you as their master.
SERVANT (*pounds with the cane*): His Excellency, the Majestic Lord and sovereign Duke Almaviva . . .
FIGARO: Protector of Virtue.
SERVANT: Master of two hundred cattle and chambermaids . . .
FIGARO: Guardian of Innocence.
SERVANT: High judge for the Inquisition.
FIGARO: Paragon of Fidelity.
SERVANT: Chief stockholder in the Gallows Manufacturing Corporation . . .
FIGARO: Nerves, don't fail me now; I've almost got him . . .
DUKE: What are you whispering there, Figaro?
FIGARO: Pardon, my Lord—the list of honors heaped upon you has taken my breath away . . . I'm speechless. (*Hoarsely*) Protector of Virtue, Guardian of Innocence, Paragon of Fidelity!
SUSANNE (*whispering to Figaro*): Let's not get carried away.
DUKE: What are you whispering there!
SUSANNE: (*hoarsely*): I was only saying how much I share my fiancé's deep respect for my lord.
DUKE: What is this sudden epidemic of laryngitis?
DUCHESS: . . . But the expression of deepest emotion. The dear people have a request, a request I find quite justified. They are deeply moved by the way you reward the virtuous and defend the innocent.
SUSANNE: Quite moved!
DUCHESS: Since you did away with the noble privilege of wedding night visitation—for my sake—you have become the object of utmost admiration.
FIGARO: Utmost.
SUSANNE: Utmost.
DUKE: Yes . . . since I did away with the "privilege," as you say, I eliminated this barbaric practice . . .
BACILLUS (*hands the Duke a note*).
DUKE (*reads*): . . . "This barbaric practice in order to place in its stead the sweet and freely given sacrifice of a loyal servant."

FIGARO: A triumph of virtue! Hurrah!
SERVANT: Hurrah! Three cheers for our lord . . . hip, hip . . .
DUKE: I am honored that my ideas regarding our manners and mores have found such unanimous approval. (*Aside—in an angry tone.*) . . . But why right now of all times . . . and why all of a sudden? What's this?
BACILLUS (*hands the Duke a note*)
DUKE (*with regained composure*): And what is the cause of this, if I may ask?
DUCHESS: Duke Almaviva, it was your wise decision that saved this poor creature (*Turning towards Susanne.*) from a night of shame and humiliation.
SUSANNE (*bows in gratitude to the Duke*): Saved by the Duke (*Turning to Figaro.*) saved . . . for him.
SERVANT: Three cheers for the virtue of our lord! Hip-hip . . .
DUCHESS: Through your upright and honest behavior, this woman may enjoy her wedding night with the lord of her heart and not with the lord of the house. Not the barbarous practice of old—but a sweet surrender, freely given . . .
SERVANT: A triumph of Virtue . . . Hip-hip
DUKE (*loudly*): Wait . . . The wedding of these two people . . .
DUCHESS: . . . will be a tender celebration indeed if you would assent to the request of these dear people to be the chosen one who will place the veil of matrimony upon their virginal heads. How fitting and proper this would be!
FIGARO (*hands the veil to the duke*).
SERVANT: Hurrah! Three cheers for the virtue of our lord, hip-hip . . .
SUSANNE: My lord, could you give us a few words of wisdom which would be appropriate to the situation? How fitting would it be for you, who are so concerned with the virtue of your chambermaids . . .
DUKE: Holy harlots in heaven. What do I do now?
FIGARO: Look at her, my lord. The beauty of this woman gives your gesture an extra grandeur . . .
SUSANNE: Appearance has nothing to do with it . . . what we are talking about is the inner glory of our lord . . .
SERVANT: Three cheers for the inner glory of our lord . . . hip-hip
DUKE: Bacillus—think of something—quick!

BACILLUS (*hands Duke another note*).
DUKE (*reading aloud*): "Stand for time" . . . . Oh?!
DUCHESS: I beg your pardon?
DUKE (*embarrassed*): The time . . . the time . . . where does it go?
DUCHESS: That's why we have to get things rolling here. Place the veil on her head so the wedding can begin—seal their marriage . . .
Figaro forces the veil into the Duke's hands.
DUKE: I place my blessing upon this marriage.
BACILLUS (*whispering*): Stall . . . stall . . .
DUKE: . . . at a more appropriate time.
DUCHESS: All we need is your word.
DUKE: This isn't the time or place for such an important event. Right. The people shall bring out their best clothes, the rooms will have to be decorated, of course. This doesn't happen everyday, you know. When two such wonderful people are joined in holy matrimony . . .
BACILLUS (*whispering*): Stall . . . stall
DUKE: When two such wonderful loving people are joined together in the act of holy matrimony . . .
BACILLUS (*whispering*): Keep it up . . .
DUKE: . . . for all eternity . . .
SERVANT: Amen.
DUKE (*to Bacillus*): These are times that try men's souls—I need a first-class . . .
BACILLUS: I know. Special Delivery. I'm on my way.
Exit Duke and Duchess.
FIGARO (*to Susanne*): Well, my sweet. We did it.
SUSANNE: If our marriage is as good as our wedding, then I predict a rosy future.
FIGARO: When I think of our future together . . . I see a kaleidoscope of color.
Exit Figaro and Susanne. Cherubin crawls out from beneath the chair.
CHERUBIN: O holy mother of Mary—blessed be your madonnal bosom. The duke's forgotten about me. What a happy event for this innocent victim of circumstance!
SERVANT (*from offstage, approaching*): His excellency the particularly high-born, well-heeled duke Almaviva, lord of two

hundred cattle and chambermaids; Count of Castille and Catalonia, high judge for the Inquisition, chief stockholder of the Gallows Manufacturing Corporation . . .
Cherubin disappears quickly under the armchair. Duke and servant appear on stage.

DUKE: Holy shit! Of all the . . . Va nella figa della butana che to ha cacata. I can finally get it off my chest! It's not enough that they eat my food and wreck my carpets now they want to rob me of my last pleasure in life. This wedding will not take place! Yes, I will not allow this wedding to take place. (*To the servant.*) Hey, you—throw that chair around a bit. I need a visible symbol of my anger!
The servant upends the armchair: Cherubin.

DUKE: Cherubin! You! Again!
CHERUBIN: Uh, I can explain everything . . .
DUKE: That's the third time . . . you're driving me crazy!
CHERUBIN: It's . . . uh . . . a silly habit of mine, my lord.
DUKE: I'll have you whipped for this.
CHERUBIN: You see, the last time I was under here . . .
DUKE: I set the dogs on you.
CHERUBIN: I heard you and Susanne speak . . .
DUKE: I'll fix you all over again.
CHERUBIN: er, speak on a certain subject . . .
DUKE: I'll have you transferred.
CHERUBIN: which the duchess . . .
DUKE: . . . to the infantry!
CHERUBIN: . . . will never know!
DUKE: . . . as an officer! You leave today. The matter's closed.
   (*Turns to go.*) A disgusting man. Holy shit.
SERVANT: His Excellency . . .
DUKE: Oh, shut up.
   Exit Duke and servant.
CHERUBIN: A disgusting man.
FIGARO (*opening a hole in one of the walls—"Laugh-In" style*): You said it, kid.
CHERUBIN: Figaro?!
FIGARO: Figaro here, Figaro there—I heard everything. By the way, congratulations on your new promotion.
CHERUBIN: No more tongue-in-cheek . . . tongue-in-ear . . . tongue-in . . . farewell Romance.

20 *A Crazy Day*

FIGARO: Wait, Cherubin! Come here for a second, friend of female pulchritude. I need you for my plan.
CHERUBIN: There are no plans left. Instead of burying my head between the arms of a French brunette, I'll be burying my head in a trench somewhere, dodging French lead. Poor me.
FIGARO: Listen, stupid. A light-hearted fool like you is s'posed to turn into a flat-footed soldier?
CHERUBIN: How else can I ease my pain?
FIGARO: Easy—all you have to do is march out: uniform, drums, the whole hero bit, you know. And when you reach the city limits duck out and tip-toe back like the good civilian that you are.
CHERUBIN: The duke will shoot me right back to my regiment.
FIGARO: You let me take care of the duke.
CHERUBIN: But it's my ass.
FIGARO: Your ass is Blanchette's business; namely, because you are going to hide out in her room. I'll fix everything.
CHERUBIN: I could kiss you, Figaro. You've saved me from a hero's death.
Cherubin kisses Figaro wildly all over the face.
FIGARO: Cut it out, willya. People will get the wrong idea.
CHERUBIN: But isn't that what's s'posed to happen? I mean, don't you know the rules of any good comedy? In a comedy everything is possible—especially the impossible! The poor get rich, the rich are betrayed, unhappy people get happy and so forth and so on. And even the guy who's got women on the brain—like a change of pace.
Cherubin kisses Figaro; Cherubin exits quickly.
FIGARO: Comedy?!

Scene change: End of Act I—Cherubin and servant spread a large tarpaulin in front of box. The two sing the following, Cherubin singing the refrain alone.

WE MARCHED ON TOWARDS TOLEDO
THE DAY BEFORE THE FIGHT
AND OUR STOMACHS GROWLED
LIKE JACKALS IN THE NIGHT.

REFRAIN:

O WHERE YOUR LOVELY, GENTLE SMILE
THOSE LIPS CARESSING ONCE MY BROW
O LADY AMID THE BATTLE'S TRIAL
DON'T KEEP THEM FROM ME NOW.

WE MARCHED ON TOWARDS TOLEDO
YOU KNOW HOW SPAIN CAN GET;
THEY BURNED OUT THE CORNFIELDS,
WE DRANK UP OUR OWN SWEAT.

WE MARCHED ON TOWARDS TOLEDO
THE SKY GREW BLACK AS DEATH
AND COLD ROSE IN THE TRENCHES
AND WE COULD SEE OUR BREATH.

WE MARCHED ON TOWARDS TOLEDO
"TOMORROW AT DAWN," WE SAID:
OUR EYES GLOWED LIKE PASSION'S FIRE
THE EASTERN SKY WAS RED.

FORWARD ON TOLEDO!
WE MOUNT THE FIRST ATTACK—
A BULLET GOT ME IN THE HEAD,
AND A SABER THROUGH THE BACK.

AND SO MY COMRADES ALL FAREWELL!
AND SO MY LOVE—ADIEU!
I GO WHERE ONLY HEROES GO
I DID IT ALL FOR YOU!

ACT TWO

The Duchess' chambers; dressing table, screen, etc.
Susanne is helping the Duchess dress.

DUCHESS: Well, what do you say now? The Duke has given us his word. The wedding *will* take place.
SUSANNE: You came just in time.
DUCHESS: Figaro told me everything: that my husband was chasing around, you know, the whole thing . . .
SUSANNE: At first he sent Bacillus with little letters; then he started showing up himself with his little "requests" . . .
DUCHESS: He doesn't love me anymore.
SUSANNE: How can you be so sure?
DUCHESS: Loneliness is a great convincer, Susanne.
SUSANNE: But he's so jealous . . .
DUCHESS: That is because he is so vain. He loves me like he loves one of his possessions . . . like he loves his gold watches. Was he ever tender to a watch, hmm? (*Softly.*) I'm tarnished anyway, and no little smiles or sweet nothings can bring that back. I hear the hour strike and strike and echo and I'm alone.
SUSANNE: Do you think Figaro will always love me?
DUCHESS: I think that men don't understand love.
SUSANNE (*sings*): I want you near
    when the silver-haired night
    kisses the dark green trees.
    The heartbeats of resting birds:
    I want to feel the world alive.
    The moon sinking down
    A green woven sea.

    I want you near
    When the petals of a rose
    Divide the dark and light

A knock is heard.
    When the petals of a rose
    Divide the dark and light.

FIGARO (*from outside*): Someone's at the door!
SUSANNE: I'm sorry, what did you say?

DUCHESS (*imitating Figaro's voice*): Someone's at the door! (*Laughing.*) Namely, Figaro.
SUSANNE: Figaro? Why didn't he say anything?
Susanne hurries to the door, opens it; Figaro enters holding his hand over his eyes.
FIGARO: I'm blinded!
DUCHESS & SUSANNE (*together*): Oh my God!
FIGARO (*taking away his hand*): . . . by your beauty, ladies! Who could look upon you and not be blinded by the brilliance of your presence?
DUCHESS: Oh, I see.
SUSANNE: Don't talk like that, you sound like the Duke.
FIGARO: Where else would it be right to talk like that—these are his rooms.
DUCHESS: Any news, Figaro?
FIGARO: I've been eavesdropping on the Duke.
SUSANNE: That's nothing new.
FIGARO: The Duke's promoted Cherubin to Lieutenant and sent him off to war.
DUCHESS: That's awful!
FIGARO: Not quite—I've hidden him in the palace.
DUCHESS: That's dangerous—you know the Duke when he gets angry.
FIGARO: Not quite so dangerous as you might think. I've thought up a disguise for the kid. A disguise which might please the Duke a great deal, in fact.
SUSANNE: What do you mean by that, Figaro?
DUCHESS: You're talking in riddles.
FIGARO: Well, listen to the answer then: the Duke's angry and intends to do all he can to stop the wedding.
DUCHESS: But he's already given the go-ahead.
FIGARO: The Duke giveth and the Duke taketh away.
SUSANNE: He won't be able to, though.
FIGARO: He might not be able to—we'll have to soothe him . . . appease him . . . make him purr just like any Catalonian cat . . .
DUCHESS: Purr?
SUSANNE: Purr?
FIGARO: Purr.
SUSANNE: You're crazy, Figaro.

FIGARO: May I finish please? Susanne will make her affections known to the Duke and arrange a private rendezvous.
SUSANNE: You are crazy, Figaro!
FIGARO: Your "change of heart" will make the Duke more inclined to allow our wedding to take place. And then, in the dark of night, when he stretches out his grubby hands for my wife . . .
SUSANNE: That's terrible, Figaro!
FIGARO: . . . Cherubin, in your clothes, will yield to his passionate embrace.
SUSANNE: That's wonderful, Figaro!
FIGARO: May I finish, please! The Duke receives the proper reward for his unfaithfulness . . .
DUCHESS: And Cherubin?
FIGARO: I'll fix it for him.
SUSANNE: He'll fix it for him, my lady, with his wit.
DUCHESS: I like it . . . But isn't it dangerous?
FIGARO: Danger, my lady, is a small price to pay to serve such beauty . . . or, as they say in America, nothing ventured, nothing gained.
DUCHESS: Then, venture, Figaro!
SUSANNE: And gain!
FIGARO: Adieu! I'll send up Cherubin. it's up to you to make a lady out of him . . . a lady that will cause the Duke's daring to swell with desire; to raise his lust to new heights; to . . .
SUSANNE: Figaro, there are ladies present!
FIGARO: From whom, I regret, I must take my leave.
Exit Figaro.
DUCHESS: What a man, your Figaro. Cherubin ought to be here any minute.
SUSANNE: He's so brave.
DUCHESS: And so handsome.
SUSANNE: And so smart.
DUCHESS: And so young!
SUSANNE (*sighs*): Figaro!
DUCHESS: Cherubin! Quick, Susanne, help me with my make-up. Are the curls OK? What about my cheeks? Too pale? My hair is a mess.
A knock.
SUSANNE: It's fine, my lady.

DUCHESS: What do you mean by that?
A second knock.
SUSANNE: The answer is waiting at the door.
Susanne answers the door; Cherubin enters.
SUSANNE: Good day, General.
CHERUBIN: Good day, Susanne.
DUCHESS: Good day, Lieutenant.
CHERUBIN: Your pardon, my lady—I'm blinded!
SUSANNE: . . . by your beauty, my lady—who could help but be blinded in the presence of such beauty. We've already heard these lines.
CHERUBIN *(to the Duchess)*: The Duke has made me a warrior, my lady. Help me, my lady.
SUSANNE: What a bold introduction!
DUCHESS: How boldly he talks! Has Figaro told you everything?
CHERUBIN: Just that you were expecting me.
DUCHESS: Good. Susanne, lock the door.
Susanne locks the door.
CHERUBIN *(puzzled)*: My lady?
DUCHESS: Yes, Lieutenant? Take off your tunic, Cherubin.
CHERUBIN *(even more puzzled)*: My Lady?
DUCHESS: Yes, Lieutenant? Susanne, take off your dress.
CHERUBIN: You really want me to take this off?
DUCHESS: And put on Susanne's dress. A masquerade, my friend.
CHERUBIN: Masquerade?
SUSANNE: The General is about to become the prettiest girl around. Now wouldn't that be nice.
CHERUBIN *(after a short pause)*: Better a make-believe girl than a real dead hero.
Susanne has taken off her dress, Cherubin his tunic.
SUSANNE: Hands up, soldier—on you knees.
Cherubin kneels, raises his arms. Susanne pulls the dress down over his head.
SUSANNE: Well, Miss—what do you think of your new clothes?
CHERUBIN: Not bad, Miss, not bad. The shoulders are a little tight the breast a little flat—do either of you ladies happen to have an extra breast handy?
SUSANNE: Sir, remember yourself!
CHERUBIN: We're all women here.
SUSANNE: He likes his new role. All the better.

CHERUBIN (*boldly; bows before Susanne*): Would the Gentlemen care to dance?
Cherubin takes Susanne and dances a few steps.
SUSANNE: My, what an impertinent female!
CHERUBIN (*to the Duchess*): Don't you think I've become awfully pale lately, Dearie?
DUCHESS: Yes, dear. I think you ought to take it easy.
CHERUBIN: You're right, dear. These constant love affairs do tire one out so. (*To Susanne.*) Susie, my left eyelid isn't quite right.
DUCHESS: Quick, Susanne, get the wig.
Susanne gets the wig; the Duchess and Susanne put make-up on Cherubin. Grimaces and laughter.
CHERUBIN: A bit more sexiness around the mouth if you please.
Susanne places the wig on Cherubin.
CHERUBIN: Not permanent wave again! Isn't there a wig with a decent style in that closet!
SUSANNE: You *are* a beauty, m'am.
CHERUBIN: Thank you. I am used to compliments.
SUSANNE: Good enough to eat.
CHERUBIN: How dare you stand here half-naked and presume to . . .
SUSANNE: What a jerk. (*She turns to go.*) I'll just put a dress on. Good-bye, ladies.
Susanne exit. Duchess and Cherubin look at each other with slight embarrassment. Pause.
DUCHESS: Well, young man?
CHERUBIN: Yes, my lady?
Silence.
DUCHESS: How're things at home?
CHERUBIN: I'm an orphan.
DUCHESS: I see.
Silence.
CHERUBIN: My lady—
DUCHESS: Yes, Cherubin?
CHERUBIN: Are you an orphan, too?
DUCHESS: I'm lonely.
CHERUBIN: Don't you have a lot of visitors?
Silence.
DUCHESS: What do the simple people think of me?

CHERUBIN: They obey you, madam.
DUCHESS: I see.
CHERUBIN: May I say something?
DUCHESS: Yes, Cherubin.
CHERUBIN: I can't right now.
  Silence.
DUCHESS: You may say it later.
CHERUBIN: You are very beautiful, my lady, I . . .
DUCHESS: Yes, Cherubin?
CHERUBIN: I can't right now.
  Silence.
DUCHESS: Do you like olives, Cherubin?
CHERUBIN: Black or green?
DUCHESS: The ones we get from the farmers.
CHERUBIN: Oh, I like the farmers and I like olives, too. I like to walk through the fields.
DUCHESS: Do the young boys still dance after the harvest?
CHERUBIN: They dance until the girls tumble down.
  Silence.
CHERUBIN: My lady?
DUCHESS: Yes, Cherubin.
CHERUBIN: I am a servant.
DUCHESS: Yes, Cherubin?
CHERUBIN: I am a young man.
DUCHESS: Yes, Cherubin.
CHERUBIN: You're so far away.
DUCHESS: Yes, Cherubin.
CHERUBIN: Can one close the gap with three steps?
  A knock. Duchess and Cherubin look at each other anxiously. Silence.
DUKE (*offstage*): Why is the door locked?
DUCHESS: Oh my God—the Duke!
CHERUBIN: The Duke? Oh my God!
DUKE (*offstage*): Open the door right now! Madam, why have you locked the door?
DUCHESS: Because I'm all alone. (*To Cherubin.*) Quick, get into the closet.
DUKE (*offstage*): Because you're alone? I can hear talking.
DUCHESS: Talking? Of course, I'm talking to you!
  Cherubin disappears into the closet; Duchess opens the door,

Duke storms in.
DUKE: Where is he?
DUCHESS: Whom do you mean?
DUKE: Him, that's whom. I heard a man's voice in here.
DUCHESS: Oh, you must mean Susanne.
DUKE: Don't you think I know the difference between a mare and a stud?
DUCHESS: You're angry for no reason, my lord. I was helping Susanne try on some wedding dresses, and when she heard your deep voice, she rushed into my closet.
DUKE: Then, let me see for myself.
DUCHESS: My clothes closet?
DUKE: The contents.
DUCHESS: My clothes? Are you interested in the latest fashions?
DUKE: Don't make me angrier than I already am! Susanne, you are to come out of there this instant!
DUCHESS: Wait, my lord. Susanne is in the process of changing her clothes—she's half naked.
DUKE: I want to see her immediately!
DUCHESS: A half-naked young girl? You have strange interest in the affairs of my chambermaid, my lord.
DUKE: The honor of a noble family is at stake, madame. Will you please leave our servants out of this!
DUCHESS: The honor of the mistress of this noble family is at stake my dear Duke. You are to stop this running around immediately.
DUKE: OK. OK. Even if she is half-naked, at least she can talk, can't she? Susanne, are you in there?
DUCHESS: Susanne, I forbid you to speak.
DUKE: You are making yourself look very suspicious, madame. We'll see about this. I'll have the door smashed in. Will you have the kindness to accompany me? I intend to have your room locked from the outside. Everything stays where it is.
DUCHESS: You are going too far, my lord!
DUKE: And you are going with me, madame.
Exit Duke and Duchess. Susanne comes out of her room.
SUSANNE: My God! Why does the duke have to come along now of all times. That adds an interesting sub-plot to this thing.
Cherubin steps out of the closet cautiously.
CHERUBIN: I won't come out of this alive. No sir, I won't come

out of this alive. If the Duke catches me one more time, I'll die an early death. I'm quitting this comedy.

SUSANNE: You have to hide, Cherubin!

CHERUBIN: Where? The Duke's already wise to the chair bit. And he's already found me behind the curtains before. He can't come across me hunched down in the closet . . . aha! I've got it—A quick leap out the window!

SUSANNE: That's too dangerous.

CHERUBIN (*moving toward Susanne; in a matter-of-fact tone*): If I am indeed about to end my life so tragically, I feel I am in need of a momentary diversion.
Cherubin kisses Susanne passionately and returns to the window sill.

CHERUBIN: Tell the Duchess . . .

SERVANT (*from offstage, approaching*): His Excellency, the particularly high-born, well-heeled Duke Almaviva . . .
Cherubin jumps; Susanne runs to the window.

SUSANNE: He made it! Such a brave man. You may fire when ready, Gridley.

SERVANT: Lord of two hundred cattle and chambermaids. High judge of . . .

DUKE: So, do you still insist on not opening that door voluntarily?

DUCHESS: Do you still insist on using force to open this door?

DUKE (*to servant*): Forward. Crowbar. Break down the door.
Servant bends down and makes ready to ram the door with his head.

SERVANT: His Excellency, the particularly high-born, well-heeled Duke . . .

DUCHESS: Wait, my lord. Behind this door you'll find Susanne and no one else. Believe me.

DUKE: Why so nervous, madame?

DUCHESS: Susanne may seem a bit . . . different

DUKE: Indeed? Different?

DUCHESS: Yes . . . perhaps a bit hairier than usual.

DUKE: Indeed? Hairier, you say?

DUCHESS: Yes, in fact her shoulders may even seem a little . . . broader than usual.

DUKE: Broad shoulders, you say?

DUCHESS: Indeed. A deep voice. You seem to be describing a

man, madame. Forward.
DUCHESS: Wait! That man is a woman . . . I mean, that woman is a man!
DUKE: Why, whatever do you mean?
DUCHESS: Spare him! He's innocent!
DUKE: Aha! Just as I thought. (*To Servant.*) Forward.
Servant runs headfirst against the door; Susanne opens door, servant runs through and runs into a dresser in the closet. Silence.
DUKE: Well, Let's see who is in this room.
SERVANT (*dazed*): His Excellency, the particularly high-born well-heeled Duke Almaviva, Lord over . . .
Servant falls over.
DUKE: Idiot.
Susanne comes merrily out of the closet.
DUKE: Susanne!?
DUCHESS: Susanne!?
SUSANNE (*glancing at the servant*): If you'll excuse me, my lord, your servant really should be more careful.
DUKE (*rushing into the closet*): There must be somebody else hiding here . . .
SUSANNE (*to the Duchess, softly*): Don't worry, madame, Cherubin's gone out through the window.
DUCHESS: Jesus! . . . thank you. Is that a load off my mind.
Duke comes out of the closet.
DUKE: Nothing! Nothing but dresses! (*To Duchess.*) But you said yourself . . .
DUCHESS: . . . that you've gone too far, my lord.
DUKE: Your delay in opening the door . . . the business with the deep voice, broad shoulders. I had every reason to think . . .
DUCHESS: You have every reason to apologize. But I won't accept your apology.
DUKE: Madame, I beg you . . . don't make a scene . . . believe me, I'm very embarrassed about the whole thing.
DUCHESS: You're embarrassed?!
DUKE: I'm sorry . . .
DUCHESS: Sorry, my lord? Perhaps now you'll think less of yourself and more of me.
DUKE: Have I ever neglected my duties?
DUCHESS: I'm not talking about your duties. You're my husband . . .

DUKE: Do you have to bring our private affairs into this . . . now of all times.
A knock at the door.
FIGARO (*offstage*): Are things about ready, ladies?
Duke throws open the door—stands eye to eye with Figaro.
FIGARO: There's just so many things that have to be done before the wedding . . . the gowns, the girls, the caterer, the band . . .
DUKE: Shut up! What are you doing here?
FIGARO: What else should a bridegroom be looking for on his wedding day?—his blushing young bride. Susanne came in here, and so—abracadabra, I follow. Susanne goes in there, I go, too. You see, my lord—you might say I'm pursuing my career goals.
DUKE: Shut up.
DUCHESS: The poor thing is all excited, my lord. Let's get on with the ceremony. Let's get on with the wedding.
DUKE: I hereby declare . . . (*Aside.*) stall, stall . . . Marcelline should be here any minute now . . . I hereby declare . . .
Duke gives sign to his servant.
SERVANT: His Excellency, the particularly high-born, well-heeled Duke Almaviva . . .
A knock.
DUKE (*aside*): There she is! (*To servant.*) Open the door.
SERVANT (*going over to the door*): Lord over two hundred cattle and chambermaids, high judge for . . .
Antonio, the gardener, throws open the door. Door slams against the servant, servant falls over. Antonio is drunk and is wearing Cherubin's wig.
ANTONIO: Ciao! (*Antonio sees the servant out cold on the floor.*) Three cheers for our host! Hip, hip . . .
DUKE: The guy's gone nuts!
ANTONIO: Antonio, my occupation; Gardener, my appellation. Dazed, not crazed. Cheers, Duchess baby—Skol, Duke-O!
DUKE: Get him outta here!
Servant stands up with difficulty and sways toward Antonio. Antonio sways toward the servant and embraces him. Slapstick.
ANTONIO (*sings*): . . ."Regrets, I've had a few . . ."
DUKE: I've never experienced anything like this in my entire life!

ANTONIO: A teetotaler, I'll bet, eh? You can toss your servants out the window easy enough, but you can't take a drink, is that it? As I always say, I say, Antonio, you should honor thy mother and Duke . . .

DUKE: I said that's enough!

ANTONIO: You're right, that is enough. (*Goes to the window.*) If he had only fallen where the weeds are it would have been okay. But I ask you—sixteen innocent young tulips? Boom! just like that, one blow.

DUKE: What's he talking about now?

ANTONIO: Oh heart of stone, you cannot feel the Gardener's pain. What kind of attitude is that to have toward your own plants? Oh, the humanity! My lord!

DUKE: Get him outta here!

ANTONIO: I'm on my way. First, allow me to cast a last sad look upon the young corpses.

Duke runs to the window and looks down into the garden.

DUKE: Who destroyed these flowers under here?

ANTONIO: Now you ask. Why, my heart bleeds in sorrow! Horrible, isn't it?

DUKE: He can't tell me anything. (*To Susanne.*) Susanne, did something fall from here?

ANTONIO: I'll answer that question. It was a woman in women's clothing . . . rather, a man in a dress, really—well, rather . . .

SUSANNE: Now he's done it.

FIGARO: Don't believe a word of it, my lord. (*To Antonio*) Antonio, how much is three times three?

ANTONIO: Seventeen, why? Seventeen, remainder four.

FIGARO: You see, my lord, drunk—totally out of it.

DUKE: But the tulips in the garden . . .

FIGARO: A duck, my lord.

DUKE: A duck?

FIGARO: Yes, a big fat duck.

DUKE: A fat duck?

FIGARO: Almost as big as a hawk.

DUKE: As big as a hawk?

FIGARO: Fell from the sky.

DUKE: Fell?

FIGARO: Horrible, isn't it?

ANTONIO: Wait a minute—you mean a hawk wearing a wig don't you, Figaro? Who's drunk around here anyway? me or you? Here, give your hawk his hair back. (*Gives Figaro the wig.*) Tell your bird Antonio says hi, and if he does that again . . .
DUKE: Whose wig is this?
DUCHESS: It belongs to me, my lord. There's an easy explanation for all of this. I got tired of looking at the thing and threw it out the window.
DUKE: A wig like this won't trample flowers, madame.
FIGARO: But a drunken gardener like that will, my lord.
ANTONIO: I won't have you casting aspersions on this innocent individual. I won't have it!
DUKE: Just what are you aiming at, Figaro?
FIGARO: It's all quite logical, my lord. The gentle Duchess, tired of having the wig clutter up her chamber, tossed it out the window. it landed below in the garden where the gardener found it. In his drunken stupor, he trampled the flowers. Q.E.D.
ANTONIO: He lies faster than I can think.
DUKE (*to Figaro*) Didn't you say something before about a hawk?
FIGARO: A hawk, my lord?
DUKE: Yes, a duck.
FIGARO: A duck, my lord?
DUKE: Yes, a big fat duck.
FIGARO: A big fat duck, my lord?
DUKE: Plummeting from the sky.
FIGARO: Plummeting?
DUKE: A swan-song, eh?
ANTONIO: A plummeting swan! That's going too far. I think you've all had too much to drink.
Meanwhile, servant has recovered—Antonio embraces him.
ANTONIO: Come, comrade—let's leave this den of iniquity . . . hawks wearing wigs . . . ducks plummeting out of the sky . . . isn't it disgusting what these people will say when they're drunk? As I always say, I say, Antonio—drink just enough to quench your thirst. You can't win 'em all.
Antonio and servant stagger off stage.
DUKE: That guy will be punished—severely.
DUCHESS: After the wedding, my lord! Now give your approval and let's get on with it!

Figaro and Susanne kneel in front of the Duke.
DUKE: I hereby declare . . .
FIGARO: Susanne!
SUSANNE: Figaro!
A knock at the door.
FIGARO: Not again! This comedy is becoming tragic.
Bacillus enters and sneaks over to the Duke.
BACILLUS *(to the Duke, softly)*: A new intrigue is ready and waiting.
DUKE: Much obliged! *(Loudly.)* Come closer, Marcelline.
Enter Marcelline.
SUSANNE: That old bag.
FIGARO: Something's up now.
DUKE: My dear Marcelline. Do you have any objection to the wedding of my manservant Figaro and my chambermaid Susanne?
MARCELLINE: I have, my lord.
DUKE *(to Bacillus)* First class work, you scoundrel!
BACILLUS: Thank you. When you think about the short space of time . . .
DUKE: Present your objection, Marcelline.
MARCELLINE *(pointing to Figaro)*: I have loaned this man three hundred dollars.
FIGARO: I know that, so what?
MARCELLINE: On the condition . . .
FIGARO: I don't know anything about . . .
MARCELLINE: . . . that he would marry me.
FIGARO: I never knew . . . My lord, it is true, this lady did loan me three hundred dollars.
DUKE: On the condition . . .
FIGARO: On the condition that I pay her back . . . your average business transaction.
MARCELLINE: He's lying, my lord. I have a right.
FIGARO: . . . to get your money back.
MARCELLINE: . . . to get you, Figaro! How I want to be your loving wife and mother to all your children!
SUSANNE: She knows no bounds of common decency, does she?
FIGARO: My lord, I swear—I never . . .
DUKE: However that may be . . . this needs to be handled by a court of law! The wedding will have to be postponed until a

later date. I'll see to the speedy conclusion of this case. (*To Bacillus.*) Get going, Bacillus, prepare the courtroom and round up the usual witnesses. (*To Marcelline.*) Come along, Marcelline. Place your trust in the court of law.
Exit: Duke, Bacillus and Marcelline.
Figaro, Susanne and Duchess remain on stage.
SUSANNE: One to nothing, the Duke.
DUCHESS: I'm sorry for you both.
FIGARO: Never fear, Figaro's here!
SUSANNE: Do you know a way out, Figaro?
FIGARO: First of all, the game isn't over yet. One inning does not make a ballgame. And with love all things are possible . . . I guess.
SUSANNE: Clichés, Figaro.
DUCHESS: Go on, Figaro.
FIGARO: First of all: the game's not over yet! We still have the hearings in court. Susanne, go to the Duke's chambers and demand a rendezvous right away. A rendezvous on one condition . . .
SUSANNE: On the condition that nothing will happen!
FIGARO: On the condition that he, as judge, will show us the appropriate evenhandedness.
DUCHESS: Seeing as he tends to like Susanne more than Marcelline, I think he'll go for it.
FIGARO: And when he shows up tonight at the agreed-upon time . . .
DUCHESS: After everything that's happened, we have to leave Cherubin out of this . . .
FIGARO: And bring you into it, my lady! You'll have to be the one inside Susanne's dress. Just keep thinking about your dear husband's promises. (*Figaro kneels.*) O beloved, let me climb to the pinnacle of my desire . . . you'll catch him red-handed, so to speak.
DUCHESS: This is getting better all the time.
FIGARO: That was part B. The duke roasted on his own grill.
SUSANNE: And part C? With love all things are possible, remember.
FIGARO: Part C has to do with parts A & B.
SUSANNE (*places a quick kiss on his left cheek*) And that has to do with your brilliance. (*A quick kiss on his right cheek.*) And

that with your bravery. (*Another kiss, left cheek.*) And that with your cunning.

FIGARO (*kisses Susanne on the mouth*): And that has to do with your beauty.

DUCHESS: What a lovely couple you two make.

Change of scene: End of Act II. Cherubin and gardener stretch a tarpaulin in front of the box. The Duchess comes forth and sings:

>   To be alone and see
>   how the day follows night follows day
>   how the hours pass by and go
>   like strangers who don't care to stay.
>
>   Do you remember that morning,
>   The sun shone bright on the sill
>   the room echoed loud with laughter;
>   And now that room is still.
>
>   Do you remember then later
>   When we sat in the cafe at noon?
>   My hand rested soft in yours;
>   How old this hand has grown.
>
>   Do you remember that evening
>   We drank more than manners allow;
>   The wine was rich and dark and red—
>   I don't drink any now.
>
>   And do you remember at midnight
>   Your lips were all over mine
>   We watched the sun coming up in the East;
>   Now my shutters are drawn till nine.
>
>   Oh, to be alone and see
>   How the day follows night follows day
>   how the hours pass by and go
>   Like strangers who don't care to stay.

ACT THREE

Reception room of the palace. Two trunks, several chairs, etc. Duke and Bacillus are visible on stage. A knock at the door. On a signal from the Duke, Bacillus climbs suddenly into one of the trunks.

DUKE (*calling out*): Someone important or just a servant?
SUSANNE (*from offstage*): An important servant.
DUKE: Enter!
Susanne enters.
SUSANNE: With your permission, my lord. The Duchess wishes to inform the Duke that the Duchess would like to speak to the Duke.
DUKE: And what would the Duchess like to say to me?
SUSANNE: The Duchess did not inform me of that, sir.
DUKE: So, you come here to tell me the Duchess informs me she has something to say to me but you don't know what that is?
SUSANNE: May I say something, my lord? That the Duchess has me inform you she has something to say to you doesn't tell me much either.
DUKE: What do you mean by that?
SUSANNE: I mean, I came to see you.
DUKE: Oh, you needed an excuse, eh?
SUSANNE: You might say that.
DUKE: Well, Susanne?
SUSANNE (*obviously embarrassed*): Well, my lord . . .
DUKE: What do you wish to tell me?
SUSANNE: What I couldn't tell you until now.
DUKE: Indeed?
SUSANNE: A precaution, my lord. When you expressed your intentions regarding me today . . .
DUKE: You were quite negative, Susanne.
SUSANNE: How could I be otherwise? Cherubin was hiding under the chair. maybe now I can make it up to you . . .
Duke moves toward Susanne.
DUKE: Indeed? Excellent . . . excellent . . .
Susanne pulls away from the Duke.
SUSANNE: How would you feel about a little walk in the park

around midnight?

DUKE: Excellent, my child. I'll be there. I'll expect you scrubbed and clean and half undressed. By the way, you don't have to say anything to Figaro.

SUSANNE: Oh, I tell him everything.

DUKE: What?

SUSANNE: Everything he needs to know. The rest is silence.

DUKE: What a delightful treat! Almaviva, I congratulate you on your culinary achievement.

SUSANNE: The dish has yet to be enjoyed, my lord.

DUKE: Susanne, remember—No walk in the park, no walk down the aisle.

SUSANNE: And vice versa: no walk down the aisle, no walk in the park. My lord, I thank you.

DUKE: Excellent, excellent . . .

Exit the Duke. Figaro climbs out of a trunk.

FIGARO (*imitating Duke*): Excellent, excellent . . . I heard everything! The Duke takes the bait!

SUSANNE: The case is as good as won, Figaro.

FIGARO: And the girl, too!

Figaro embraces Susanne.

SUSANNE (*laughingly retreating*): Get away!

FIGARO: Ah, just one kiss . . .

SUSANNE (*seriously*): Oh, Figaro, If we can just stay together, everything will be all right.

Figaro embraces Susanne.

SUSANNE: Do you have to start this again!

FIGARO: But you said yourself, if we can only . . .

SUSANNE: What?

FIGARO: . . . stay together!

Laughing, the two exit; Bacillus climbs out of the second trunk.

BACILLUS: Excellent, excellent . . . I heard everything. Intrigues wherever you look. I must inform the Duke immediately.

Duke enters.

BACILLUS: My lord, I wish to report a new intrigue.

DUKE: Did I order a new one?

BACILLUS: Your competition, my lord. You see, as you and Susanne discussed a certain topic . . .

DUKE: You were eavesdropping!

BACILLUS: And Figaro, too!
DUKE: Figaro, too!?
BACILLUS: While I lay in this trunk, Figaro hid in that one.
DUKE: Then he heard everything!
BACILLUS: When he climbed out of that trunk, I remained in this one.
DUKE: Then you heard everything!
BACILLUS: If I may quickly recapitulate, my lord. Figaro climbed out of that trunk and said, "Excellent."
DUKE: Those were my last words!
BACILLUS: And his first.
DUKE: Pure slapstick.
BACILLUS: Then Figaro said to Susanne: "You did a good job." Then Susanne said to Figaro: "The case is as good as won." Then Figaro said to Susanne: "Give me a kiss." Then Susanne said to Figaro: "Get away." Then they . . .
DUKE: The oldest trick in the book.
BACILLUS: An antique.
DUKE: And I thought Susanne really liked me. Well, what do you expect from servants nowadays—they're all dishonest. Quick, Bacillus, a counter-intrigue.
BACILLUS: You must find Figaro guilty, my lord.
DUKE: But then how do I keep Susanne?
BACILLUS: With my next intrigue. Susanne will beg you not to make Figaro marry Marcelline. She'll beg you on her hands and knees. And you say OK.
DUKE: I say no!
BACILLUS: You say yes! under one condition: that she says yes to your conditions.
DUKE: And what exactly are my conditions?
BACILLUS: Unconditional Surrender . . . before the wedding.
DUKE: Good work, Scoundrel! . . . That's one for the books.
BACILLUS: Intrigues for the Wealthy, Volume 4, under "Intrigues for Home and Garden," page twenty-one.
DUKE: Who writes those books anyway?
BACILLUS: A Monsieur Baron de Beaumarchais of Paris.
DUKE: Hasn't he got any money? Can't he afford to put on his own intrigues?

Don Guzman di Stibizia, servant of justice and Zettelkopf, servant of Don Guzman enter.

40 A Crazy Day

Don Guzman: Don Guzman di Stibizia, servant of justice and servant.
Zettelkopf: Zettelkopf—at your service.
Duke (*to Guzman*): Why does the servant of justice need a servant, too?
Don Guzman: Because having a servant makes you a master, my lord.
Duke: If one is a master, then, why does one call oneself a servant? As in—servant of justice?
Don Guzman: Because I, as a servant of justice, earn a salary; while I, as a master, must pay a salary.
Duke: OK, Judge. You know what you have to do, don't you? The case is like this: I run the thing in order to give it the illusion of a fair trial, see? And above all, you find Figaro guilty.
Don Guzman: I understand. Above all, justice must be preserved.
Duke (*to Bacillus*): He doesn't quite understand.
Bacillus (*makes the dollar sign*): You'll have to explain things a bit more clearly.
Duke: I get it—cash.
Zettelkopf: Let me make a note of that: cash.
Don Guzman: I understand . . . the appearance of justice must be preserved at all costs. That will require more work, of course. Threefold expansion of transcripts, fourfold addition to closing remarks, fivefold rearrangement of evidence.
Duke: Don't talk so much. Just name the price.
Don Guzman: Your average court case usually runs . . .
Duke: Fifty bucks, cash—and no receipts, okay?
Zettelkopf: Let me make a note of that . . . fifty.
Don Guzman: Of course that's only the simplest of all judicial procedures . . . then you have your right to appellate court, etcetera. On the other hand, a favorable decision . . .
Duke: Sixty bucks, no more.
Zettelkopf: Let me make a note of that . . . sixty.
Don Guzman: . . . is much more desirable even if you have to include certain extras like paying witnesses—first-class perjurers—and all the other extras that you have to include . . .
Duke: On hundred bucks—my final offer.
Don Guzman: Congratulations, my lord. And might I add that the exquisite form of the judge's final judgment is all the rage

among true gentlemen of rank and wealth. My lord has excellent taste.
ZETTELKOPF (*hands Duke paper and pen*): At your service, your excellency.
DUKE: Now what does this servant's servant want?
BACILLUS: This asshole's asshole.
DON GUZMAN: The contract, my lord. A mere formality.
DUKE (*reads*): "One decision (deluxe): one hundred dollars—plus ten per cent intrigue tax: ten dollars; plus bending-the-rules-tax: fifteen dollars; perjury bonus: eleven dollars; conscience insurance: two-fifty. Grand total: one hundred thirty-eight dollars and fifty cents." What is all this?
DON GUZMAN: The extras aren't included in the original price, my lord.
DUKE: You run a hard bargain, your honor.
DON GUZMAN: Justice has its price, my lord.
Duke prepares to sign.
DON GUZMAN: At your service, my lord.
ZETTELKOPF: At your service, my lord.
Duke signs.
DUKE: There. Okay, let's go, your honor—provide the services I just paid for. Now, Figaro, let's see you get out of this one. The verdict is . . .
BACILLUS: Marriage to Marcelline . . . for life.
DUKE: And the only condition for parole?
BACILLUS: Susanne's immediate surrender. Unconditional.
DUKE: You get what you pay for, by God. I love practicing law.
Exit Duke and Bacillus.
ZETTELKOPF: A good customer.
DON GUZMAN: A good contract. One hundred big ones. Gross and net.
ZETTELKOPF: That's net and gross.
DON GUZMAN: It's gross and net.
ZETTELKOPF: I believe it's net and gross.
DON GUZMAN: Damn! It's gross and net.
Zettelkopf hands judge paper and pen.
DON GUZMAN: What am I supposed to do with this?
ZETTELKOPF: Figure up expenses. The amounts are to be subtracted from the net and transferred to the account of Zettelkopf, scribe. Ten per cent hush money—that's thirteen

dollars, fifty; plus commission from blackmail fund, plus union tax—eleven dollars.
DON GUZMAN: Since when does the employer pay the union tax?
ZETTELKOPF: An everyday occurrence, your honor.
DON GUZMAN: OK. But why did you figure more for conscience insurance?
ZETTELKOPF: What happens when the master's conscience bothers him? It's the servant who pays in the end.
DON GUZMAN: Zettelkopf, where did you get this lust for money all of a sudden?
Don Guzman picks up pen.
ZETTELKOPF: At your service, your honor.
Don Guzman signs.
ZETTELKOPF: At your service, your honor.
Marcelline and Bartholo enter.
DON GUZMAN (*bows*): At your service, madame. Don Guzman di Stibizia, servant of justice.
ZETTELKOPF: Zettelkopf, at your service, madame.
MARCELLINE: Ah, the judge. I have been looking for you everywhere. Your honor, you must help me regain what is rightfully mine.
ZETTELKOPF (*softly*): Our customers, your honor.
MARCELLINE: This is my lawyer, your honor, Dr. Bartholo.
DON GUZMAN: Ah, a colleague! Justus shustus vibus bibus.
BARTHOLO: Sossolala.
DON GUZMAN: Habemus interessum procentum.
BARTHOLO: Percentium habemus interessum!
DON GUZMAN: Ventum percentum?
BARTHOLO: Quarantum percentum!
DON GUZMAN: Trentum percentum. Basta zasta.
BARTHOLO: Bonum.
DON GUZMAN: Punctum.
MARCELLINE: What are you gentlemen discussing? It's Greek to me.
ZETTELKOPF: I beg your pardon: Latin.
DON GUZMAN (*to Marcelline*): What can I do for you, madame?
MARCELLINE: I want to marry Figaro, that's all.
DON GUZMAN: Do you have a written marriage agreement?
MARCELLINE: All I have is his IOU . . . and the promise of his excellency, the Duke.

DON GUZMAN (*takes paper*): A certain Mr. Figaro owes you three hundred dollars. Nothing else.
BARTHOLO: And suppose there were a written promise of marriage added to that? I mean, just suppose there were . . .
DON GUZMAN: A written promise added to this would, of course, necessitate added court costs, colleague.
MARCELLINE: Name your price.
DON GUZMAN: You could have your average no-frills addition at, say, thirty dollars?
ZETTELKOPF: I'll make a note of that: thirty dollars.
BARTHOLO: I'd be sure and get the best addition possible, madame. Something iron-clad.
DON GUZMAN: My opinion exactly. In that case, you would want the notarized addition, known as the "double counterfeit." That would be sixty dollars.
ZETTELKOPF: Let me get all of this down: sixty dollars, "double counterfeit."
MARCELLINE: What do you think, Doctor Bartholo?
BARTHOLO: I think you ought to grab it, madame. The addition seems to be necessary and the price is right.
MARCELLINE: OK. Sixty dollars it is.
DON GUZMAN: Congratulations, madame. And I might add that this type of addition is all the rage now with the ladies of rank and wealth.
MARCELLINE (*pays immediately*): Gentlemen, I place my fate in your hands.
DON GUZMAN: You can place your trust in the judicial process.
Marcelline turns to go.
BARTHOLO: My commission, colleague?
Don Guzman hands him some money.
DON GUZMAN: To your health.
BARTHOLO: To *our* health, colleague.
Exit Marcelline and Bartholo; enter Figaro.
DON GUZMAN: Do you have any business with these hearings, young man?
FIGARO: In all of them, your honor. I'm the defendant.
DON GUZMAN: Excellent, sir. (*To Zettelkopf.*) Our next customer. (*To Figaro.*) What kind of verdict do you expect, if I may ask?
FIGARO: A fair verdict.

ZETTELKOPF: Should I take any of this down?
DON GUZMAN: Of course, of course. But I mean in the execution of the decision . . .
FIGARO: Just and lawful.
ZETTELKOPF: Should I take that down?
DON GUZMAN: Yes, yes. Of course. (*To Figaro.*) But I mean what do you expect the witnesses to say . . .
FIGARO: The truth.
ZETTELKOPF: Should I write *that* down?
DON GUZMAN: Sir, I don't think you quite understand . . . I am prepared to offer you a modern, dynamic decision at a price you can afford.
FIGARO: I'll place my trust in the judicial process. That's free.
DON GUZMAN: Guilty!
ZETTELKOPF: Not guilty by reason of insanity!
DON GUZMAN: It serves him right.
Exit Figaro; enter Bacillus.
BACILLUS: My lord sends me to inquire whether everything is ready.
DON GUZMAN: Alea facta est.
ZETTELKOPF: His honor says that everything is ready.
Enter all: Duke, Marcelline, Bartholo, Figaro, servants. All take their places. Duke stands. All stand. Duke sits. All sit. Bacillus hands Duke a slip of paper.
DUKE (*reads*): "Agreed: one decision deluxe . . ." (*To Bacillus.*) Idiot! I declare these hearings in session. (*To Guzman.*) You may begin.
DON GUZMAN: (*to Zettelkopf*): You may begin.
ZETTELKOPF (*to court servant*): You may begin.
DON GUZMAN: First, we shall have the reading of the contents of the plaintiff's charge.
ZETTELKOPF (*opening a large file folder, reads*): Hear ye, hear ye, case no. 234-22B-1234 section 435C, paragraph 87.8 of the judicial code 3456789 . . .
DUKE (*to Guzman*): et cetera . . .
DON GUZMAN: Et cetera! The plaintiff Marcelline Krautmesser y Barbara y Fiorita y Benedetta y Mandolina y Nicolina y Pepperina y Carmen . . . a virgin of legal age . . .
VOICE: Objection!
DUKE (*to Don Guzman*): Order in the court!

DON GUZMAN (*to Zettelkopf*): Order in the court!
ZETTELKOPF (*to court servant*): Order in the court!
SERVANT: Silentium, if you please.
ZETTELKOPF (*reads*): . . . the plaintiff, Marcelline Krautmesser y Barbara y Fiorita y Benedetta y Mandolina y Pepperina y Carmen . . . bla, bla . . . hereby brings her suit against the Defendant: Figaro y . . . ? There's no other name here.
FIGARO: Figaro.
DON GUZMAN: First name?
FIGARO: Figaro.
DON GUZMAN: Are you trying to pull my leg?
FIGARO: Oh, I couldn't do that your honor.
DUKE: The old boy seems to feel pretty confident. (*To Don Guzman.*) Let's get on with it.
DON GUZMAN: Let's get on with it. (*To Figaro.*) Your social standing?
FIGARO: Accidental.
DON GUZMAN: Since when is that a social standing?
FIGARO: Since all standing is accidental. You see, if I had only been born in a fancier bed, I would have accidentally been born into a wealthy family and would have—accidentally—enough money to smooth over the accidents of justice.
DUKE (*to Don Guzman*): Enough already.
DON GUZMAN: Enough already.
SERVANT (*to Figaro*): That'll be enough out of you.
ZETTELKOPF (*continues to read*): "The suit of the aforementioned virgin of legal age, Marcelline Krautmesser y Barbara y Fiorita y . . . y . . . y Carmen objections being made against the marriage of the aforementioned Figaro Figaro. The aforementioned young Miss Marcelline will be represented by the respected, very respected respectable Dr. Bartholo."
Bartholo stands, bows deeply, sits again.
ZETTELKOPF: The aforementioned Figaro Figaro . . .
Figaro stands, sits.
ZETTELKOPF: . . . will be represented by the aforementioned Figaro Figaro.
Figaro stands.
FIGARO: Which, in plain English, means I shall represent myself.
BARTHOLO: Objection! He must have a lawyer! It can't be done without a lawyer.

FIGARO: What is always done, Dear Dr. Bartholo, can easily be undone. (*To the court.*) What good is a lawyer to me when he knows more about the intrigues of the legal system than about hard reality that surrounds us? A man who would sell his own sweat if it would help his case; who measures the effectiveness of his argument by the size of his commission! Such a gentleman, gentlemen, clothes the odious odor of his greed with the plush corduroy of expensive waistcoats.
DUKE (*to Don Guzman*): Outrageous!
DON GUZMAN (*to Zettelkopf*): Outrageous!
ZETTELKOPF (*to Servant*): Outrageous!
SERVANT: He has a point, you know.
FIGARO: If you will permit me to present my case as briefly as possible . . .
DON GUZMAN: You've already said too much. As the defendant in this case you've only to speak when spoken to.
FIGARO: The defendant rests his case. As lawyer for the defense, I would like to make one last remark . . .
DON GUZMAN: I would like to remark that your constant remarks are interrupting the progress of this hearing.
FIGARO: I only intended to precipitate the course of justice, your honor.
DON GUZMAN: Let's get on with the reading of the evidence.
ZETTELKOPF (*reads*) "Exhibit A: I, the undersigned Figaro, hereby confirm that I have received a sum of three hundred dollars from the young Miss Marcelline, etc, etc, which I promise to repay . . .
FIGARO: That's right.
ZETTELKOPF: " . . . as I marry her." Notarized signatures follow.
FIGARO: False. There was never a word about any marriage.
BARTHOLO: Oh, honorable judge, your honor! Once again a shocking case of the base immorality in which the youth of today buries its head. Here, a young, unscrupulous man promises marriage to an innocent, unwitting mature young woman.
FIGARO: Objection! The signatures are forged.
ZETTELKOPF: I repeat: the signatures are notarized.
Zettelkopf hands Don Guzman the document. Don Guzman hands it to Duke.
DUKE: Looks official to me.

Duke returns the document to Don Guzman.
DON GUZMAN: Everything in order. The signatures are genuine.
FIGARO: Counterfeit!
DUKE: As the Appellate Judge of Castille, I say the signatures are genuine. Does he want to question the decision of a Spanish Magistrate? I'll have him flogged.
FIGARO: My lord, might makes right. In other words, you have the power to be right.
BARTHOLO: We demand immediate gratification of the terms of the agreement. Marry her and pay up!
FIGARO (*aside*): Warriner's Grammar, don't fail me now! (*To the court.*) And we demand the terms of the agreement to be examined in intimate detail.
DON GUZMAN: Just what do you mean by that?
FIGARO: What are the terms exactly? That I pay back three hundred dollars. In other words—as soon as I pay as soon as I marry. And since I am not marrying, I don't need to pay.
BARTHOLO: And we affirm that the word "as" carries exactly the same meaning as that well-known coordinating conjunction "and." In short, pay and marry.
FIGARO: And I affirm that it does not function here as a coordinating conjunction but rather as a relative preposition in the temporal case: in short, as soon as I marry her, I shall have to pay up.
ZETTELKOPF (*to Don Guzman*) Coordinating conjunction or relative preposition in the temporal case?
DON GUZMAN (*to the Duke*): Coordinating conjunction or relative preposition in the temporal case?
DUKE: Coordinating conjunction or relative preposition in the temporal case?
Bacillus whispers something to Duke.
DUKE (*to Don Guzman*): Sit on it and twirl.
DON GUZMAN (*to Zettelkopf*): Sit on it and twirl.
ZETTELKOPF (*to Figaro and Bartholo*): The gentlemen are requested to view the facts of the case from a new perspective.
BARTHOLO: My pleasure! How is it so well put in that document? "Which I promise to repay." That's the same as if I were to say: "Your health will return as soon as a doctor gives you medicine." In other words, "as soon as the doctor gets here you get well . . ." Conjunction.

FIGARO: Wrong again. It goes like this: "You'll fade off as one of these doctors fades in!" In other words, "as the doc arrives, you'll be departing." Preposition.
BARTHOLO: And I say conjunction!
FIGARO: And I say preposition! Preposition!
BARTHOLO: Sir, you choose to insult me?
FIGARO: Sir, I am merely attempting to defend myself.
BARTHOLO: Gentlemen, if it please the court—I move the marriage contract be examined and accepted into evidence as Exhibit A.
DUKE: Sustained.
DON GUZMAN: Sustained.
ZETTELKOPF: Settled.
FIGARO: And what about my motion to postpone the examination of the marriage contract?
DUKE: Overruled.
DON GUZMAN: Overruled.
ZETTELKOPF: Forget it.
DUKE: The decision—I want to hear the decision.
DON GUZMAN: Of course, the decision. In a minute. In the name of God, the King of Spain, His excellency the Duke Almaviva and, by the way, in the name of justice for all, we wish to declare the following decision: The party of the first part must repay the party of the second party the sum of three hundred dollars as . . .
BARTHOLO: Conjunction.
ZETTELKOPF: . . . the party of the first part is to marry the party of the second part.
DUKE: Without delay.
DON GUZMAN: Of course, on the spot—now.
MARCELLINE: This is the happiest day of my life. (*To Figaro*) My love!
FIGARO: What? Me marry this smoke-cured Lady of lox? My lord, do you really intend to sacrifice a young, innocent servant to the arms of a wrinkled rag of ruin?
Figaro's speech is accompanied by laughter from the others.
DUKE: Well, now who's fallen into his own trap, eh?
FIGARO: I'll pay back the three hundred dollars—even if I have to get a job and work to do it! But for God's sake, don't throw me into the jaws of that Siberian Hyena. Think of Susanne, my lord. I'm sure she'd be *most* thankful.

DUKE: I'm sure she will find just the proper means to express her thankfulness. You are to marry Marcelline! Court adjourned!
FIGARO: Wait! You can't make me marry that old grandmother! I love Susanne.
BARTHOLO: It's not a laughing matter anymore, eh, Figaro?
DUKE: I said, court adjourned. The chambers are to be prepared for the wedding immediately.
FIGARO: You'll kill me just as if you took a dagger and . . .
Laughter.
FIGARO: I'll take that laughter and turn it back on you. Give me room! Elbow room! Spanish justice has miscarried! The Duke has raped the Goddess of Justice! Now we'll smash your brains against the wall! Blood runs free in the streets! We'll use your guts to write "long live the king" until the sun sets in a crimson sky! I love Susanne—do you get me! That girl has eyes as clear as still water. I'll destroy them, I'll destroy you!
Exit all. Susanne and Duchess enter.
SUSANNE: They found him guilty, madame!
DUCHESS: Guilty?
SUSANNE: He's to marry Marcelline tonight.
DUCHESS: I don't understand.
SUSANNE: Oh, I understand quite well. The Duke has lost his appetite for his chambermaids.
DUCHESS: I don't believe that. Didn't you promise to see my husband tonight?
SUSANNE: At midnight. In the park. Help us, madame!
DUCHESS: Relax, Susanne—We haven't lost yet.
SUSANNE: Yet? It's night already. What's happened to my wedding day?
DUCHESS: We must try everything. Go to the Duke right now and ask him to let Figaro go.
SUSANNE: He'll say no.
DUCHESS: He'll say yes if you do what he wants.
SUSANNE: He'll want to wait to do what he wants to do.
DUCHESS: Say yes. Tell him you'll wait for him in the park right now. Meanwhile, I'll hide. Susanne, I'll need your dress.
SUSANNE: I'm afraid, madame.
DUCHESS: You must be strong, Susanne.
Exit Susanne and Duchess. Enter Duke and Bacillus. The room

is being decorated.

BACILLUS: Susanne ought to be here any minute now, my lord.
DUKE: "Like sands in the hourglass, so run the days of our lives."
BACILLUS: Anticipation excites the appetite!
DUKE: I don't have an appetite to wait.
BACILLUS: And how does my lord intend to carry out the act of copulation?
DUKE: First, she must be punished—tastefully.
BACILLUS: Ah, a tasteful punishment.
DUKE: Then I shall tear her clothes from her body.
BACILLUS: How original.
DUKE: I hope she doesn't have any bugs or lice on her.
BACILLUS: Best to be careful.
DUKE: Then—legs spread.
BACILLUS: How gallant!
DUKE: Then, forward, cavalry attack! Hop!
BACILLUS: Hop!
DUKE: Olé!

Knock. On signal from the Duke, Bacillus disappears into a trunk. Enter Susanne.

DUKE: Ah, Susanne! Come closer. How do you like the flowers and decorations?
SUSANNE: They remind me of a funeral, my lord.
DUKE: Today is a wedding. My servant, Figaro, is marrying Marcelline. I want see smiling faces.
SUSANNE: When you take my bridegroom away, you give me little reason to smile. Let him go, my lord. He's *my* husband—it's *my* wedding.
DUKE: This is an impertinence that I cannot bear.
SUSANNE: I love him. When he looks at me my heart stops. There are no shackles in his look. He's stronger than the night. He can move heaven and earth.
DUKE: Keep going, Susanne, I'm enjoying this.
SUSANNE: What can you know about the kind of love I'm talking about?
DUKE: Now, now—let's stick to the subject. Did you scrub yourself well this morning?
SUSANNE: Like a stairway at Easter. My lord need but climb up a flight.
DUKE: Forward, Almaviva!

SUSANNE: Wait, my lord! Let Figaro go—and I'll see you in the park.
Duke comes closer.
SUSANNE: Wouldn't you care to be out in the fresh summer night air, rather than in this stuffy room?
DUKE: I want to put an end to this comedy, my child. Stay where you are.
SUSANNE: And you, too, my lord . . . or I'll scream!
DUKE: Then Figaro will have to scream, too.
SUSANNE: Figaro? What did he ever do to you? What are you going to do to him?
DUKE: Nothing . . . if you do what I want.
SUSANNE: And if I refuse?
DUKE: I like Figaro's wit; I'll have to think up a witty punishment for him.
SUSANNE: This marriage with Marcelline is witty enough.
DUKE: But not quite witty enough. We still need thirty lashes with a cat-o-nine-tails across the back of your dear fiancé.
SUSANNE: Your wit is so powerful, my lord, that sometimes it's difficult to see the wit for the power.
DUKE: Well, what'll it be?
SUSANNE: It's cold. I look at you and my blood runs cold.
DUKE: Yes or no. Consider your answer well, if you care so much for the welfare of that little creep in there.
SUSANNE: Here, take it. The meat is scrubbed. Take it. My thighs are fresh. Lick the sweat from my nipples. Go ahead—trample the garden. Oh, Figaro . . .
DUKE: This is no fun—you have to resist.
SUSANNE: Figaro, think of the spring—all flowers die to bloom again.
Duke strikes Susanne with the whip. Susanne glares at Duke.
SUSANNE: I hate you. Your blood is cold. You are already dead—even if you kill me first. You are already rotting away. You and your kind carry your guts in your hands. (*She laughs.*) Go ahead, hit me! Hit me! The pain makes me feel alive.
DUKE: Your humor—your humor, your humor—where on earth has it gone?
Duke begins to strike Susanne with force. Figaro enters from a side door. He jumps on the Duke and strangles him with the whip. Figaro and Susanne stare blankly at each other.

FIGARO: We have to get out of here. He's dead.
SUSANNE: Dead?
FIGARO: Away from here as quickly as possible.
SUSANNE: Dead? But where, Figaro?
FIGARO: I don't know . . . I don't know.
> *Figaro and Susanne exit. Duchess enters. She is wearing Susanne's dress from the earlier scene.*

DUCHESS: Susanne's dress fits perfectly. Our figures are exactly the same. It's almost time for me to be in the park . . . then my lord, we'll see the fiery lover make his advances on the innocent young maiden. We'll see the passion that he has withheld so long from his own wife . . .
> *She sees the Duke.*

DUCHESS: My lord? Almaviva? Pedrito?
> *Duchess kneels beside corpse. She places her head upon his chest. Silence.*

DUCHESS: It was s'posed to be a comedy. I wear Susanne's dress and you meet me in the Garden. You tell me how much you love me. I keep silent. Pedrito, why aren't you saying anything?

DUCHESS: It's me, Susanne. My body is young and fresh, touch it. Come closer, this girl is waiting for you. I would like you to kiss me, my lord . . . his lips don't move. I have a dead duke as a lover. A dead man. Do you remember the songs you sang under my window? I received your songs with these open arms; I felt your desire in my fingertips. You could always be so happy, so playful. Those days when I first came to this palace. Then they made me a wife. Your wife. In your house. *(Growing upset.)* Yes. Your house, your palace. Your servants, your horses, your chambermaids—your money. You made me into a Duchess. Your wife has an ass, too, Almaviva. Even when she has to dutifully hide it under layers of expensive clothes. I yearn for the arms of your servants. My lady wishes? I am ridiculous, aren't I? You are indeed beautiful, madame. I have a friend, too. It excites him just to look at me. I can feel his desire in my fingertips.
> *Cherubin enters from a back door. He sees the Duchess; she blocks the corpse from his line of vision.*

CHERUBIN: Ah. Susanne. The Goddess of the entire palace staff. The cream in the gray, mundane coffee of life. I yearn for a

taste of your sweet lips. Why don't you say something? I've been hiding out at Blanchette's for hours. In a cleaning closet. I don't want to spend my life with a bunch of old brooms. My arms and legs have gone to sleep. Kiss me, Susanne, and wake them up again.
Duchess laughs hysterically.
CHERUBIN: Oh, my lady—forgive . . . me I didn't know.
DUCHESS: Do you know who you remind me of, Cherubin? (*She points to the Duke.*) . . . Pedrito.
CHERUBIN: Is the Duke resting?
DUCHESS: Yes, Cherubin, he's resting—as usual.
CHERUBIN: Mother of Mercy! The Duke . . .
DUCHESS: Yes, Cherubin?
CHERUBIN: He's dead!
DUCHESS: Indeed? Are you sure? And I thought I heard him snoring.
CHERUBIN: Who . . . did this, madame?
DUCHESS: Do you find me attractive, Cherubin?
CHERUBIN: You? . . . You are a most enchanting woman. He's dead, madame.
DUCHESS: Why don't you kiss me. My husband won't mind.
CHERUBIN: Someone could come in at any minute. They'll find us here.
DUCHESS: Then let's go away . . . far away.
CHERUBIN: You want to leave the palace?
DUCHESS: Have you forgotten the peasants? the harvest? the olives? What do you say, Cherubin? They dance and dance and dance until the girls fall into their arms. I'd like to dance.
CHERUBIN: Dance? Do you realize what it's like to live with peasants? The soil is rocky, every vine, every olive tree is watered with the sweat of their brow. But the harvest belongs to the Duke. Dance? Sure, they dance all right. They dance so that they get so dizzy they can forget things for awhile.
DUCHESS: I can work, Cherubin.
CHERUBIN: What for? So that you can get wrinkled and bent down before your time—just like they do?
DUCHESS: I want to live, Cherubin!
CHERUBIN: Live? This is life right here, madame. Pictures on the wall, Gobelins, fine clothes, continental breakfasts . . . a

college education . . . money . . . clothes . . . servants . . . life . . . life . . .
DUCHESS: I hear my husband, the Duke.
CHERUBIN: Your husband is dead, madame. You are a widow . . . yet too young to remain a widow for long.
DUCHESS: Go . . . go . . . get out!
Cherubin exits quietly.
DUCHESS: Get out . . . no, stay here with me, Cherubin! Stay, please stay. (*In a different tone of voice.*) What I must look like! I have to change my clothes. What shall I wear this evening?
Duchess exits. Bacillus climbs out of the trunk. He sees the Duke and laughs. He plunders the body.
BACILLUS: Another intrigue, if you please? My lord need but command. My lord is a most impressive corpse. His Excellency, the particularly high-born, well-heeled Duke Almaviva. And pretty soon . . . *rigor mortis.* (*Screams:*) Murder! Manslaughter! Revolution! Revolution!
All players appear on stage. They are hidden behind the tarpaulin with which they cover the open end of the box. They let the tarpaulin fall.

CURTAIN

END

Joseph and Mary

Time: This play takes place on the evening of December twenty-fourth.

Place: The salesfloor of a large department store.

Dramatis personae: Mary, sixty-five years old; a cleaning woman. Joseph, sixty-eight years old; security guard.

Setting: I have two concepts. First, an arena-like stage: in the middle, the sales floor. Mountains of goods displayed in all their Christmas glory. At the beginning of the play the audience moves through the sales floor and takes their seats to the left and right of the stage. The curtain should remain open from the beginning. The sales floor on stage should not be depicted realistically. I imagine a more fantastical setting, which would better express the glut and unrestrained trivialization and commercialization of all things having to do with the Christmas season. Bottles, cans, manger-scenes, beds, mirrors, angels, meat, lamps—everything has been thrown together.

Concerning the production: I ask that the director not depict the two individuals in this play in a ludicrous manner. The aspect of their ridiculousness should not be ridiculous; their sorrow and their tragedy should not be played sorrowfully or tragically. The two elderly characters here have already lived so long with their individual traits that they take these as given. The predictability and the attempt to break out of this predictability is the theme of this play.

Stage: On the salesfloor goods glaringly pronounce their seasonal splendor. Hams, Jesus Christ figures, furniture, bottles, shepherds shine out in all variations of colors. In the background one sees a door with the sign, "Public Address System Control Room." While the audience takes its seat, announcement of various store specials play over the PA system.

Suggested text for announcements: Attention shoppers, boneless ham, finest quality only forty cents per pound; Hungarian

Christmas goose, exceptionally lean and tasty, only fifty-five cents per pound; shoppers, decorate your holiday table with mood-setting dripless Christmas candles, and for those candles may we suggest our beautiful star-shaped candle-holders—on sale now for only ninety-nine cents apiece, when you buy our economical ten-pack. You save thirty-five cents under our normal price. Now, for a limited time only, our perfect Christmas dinner carving set or electric carver with adjustable bone cutter for your holiday carving ease and pleasure. And now, for a limited time only: battery-operated manger scenes—the entire Holy Family, illuminated as never before for your holiday pleasure: Jesus, Mary and Joseph are included and, at no extra charge, the three wise men, three sheep and two donkeys. The entire manger scene, of course, in durable unbreakable plastic. Let the star of Bethlehem shine over your manger today. Our manger scenes come in three convenient sizes—small, for the young couple on the way up; medium for the most intimate of family celebrations, and large, for all the children and grandchildren to share in the magic of Christmas. For those more mature families whose children will not be home for the holidays we recommend the small manger set—for a holiday season you'll never forget.

(*Christmas music. After a small bit of static from the PA system, a different voice, a new announcement is heard.*)

May I have your attention please for an important announcement concerning all store employees. Repeat. Your attention please for an important announcement for all store employees. This is the Director of Personnel speaking. I would like to thank our salesmen and women on behalf of our Chairman for their tireless efforts in the service of our customers and we wish them and their families a celebration. We would like to show our appreciation for all that our employees have done this past year by giving them a small token of our thanks: a bottle of our finest quality brandy awaits all of you at the employees' exit. This gift is extended to all of our employees with the exception of our accounting department, temporary custodial workers and our non-citizen employees.

(Christmas music. The light changes slowly from bright, harsh light into a cold neon. Silence. An old woman enters the stage. She has been, quite obviously, at the hairdresser's; she wears make-up, carries a coat, and holds a large paper bag in her hand. She moves toward a couch, putting the paper bag away. She takes three packages, wrapped in Christmas wrapping out of the bag and places them on the couch. She takes off her coat, her shoes and dress. She stands in her underclothes. Then, from the paper bag, she takes her work clothes: dress, shoes, bandana; she dresses for work. First, the dress, then the shoes and finally the bandana. She sets the bandana about her head in a manner common to all cleaning women. She takes a wallet from her coat and puts it in the pocket of her cleaning smock. She regards herself in the mirror, moves closer to the mirror, looks at her face, takes out a paper tissue, dampens it with her own saliva and wipes the make-up from her face. She moves to the couch and looks down at the three Christmas packages. She folds her dress and places it in the paper bag along with the three packages. She moves behind the stage. Silence. She returns to the stage with a bucket, scrub-brush and rags. She begins to work, wiping the floor with a damp rag. Silence. She stands in front of a row of shelves, stops working, looks around her as if she were watching someone, takes a bottle of brandy from the display shelf and looks at the bottle. She places the bottle next to the display shelf and continues her work. She mops the floor in front of the PA system sound booth. She stops working again; looks about somewhat sheepishly, then, enters the booth. Silence. Then, the loudspeaker comes alive with the sound of static.)

MARY'S VOICE: Our temporary custodial workers are exempted from the traditional Christmas gift of brandy. As if we didn't do our work here, too. I'm just telling it like it is.
(Silence.)
MARY'S VOICE: Willie.
(Silence.)
MARY'S VOICE: Willie? This is your mother speaking. Do you hear me? Merry Christmas, Willie.
(Silence.)

MARY'S VOICE: And Merry Christmas to your wife and son, as well. I wish you all a very Merry Christmas.
(*Silence.*)
MARY'S VOICE: Willie! (*almost shouting*) Willie!
(*An older man in the uniform of a night watchman enters the stage. He carries a kind of knapsack over his shoulder and a bundle of keys in his hand. He hears the woman's voice from the PA system, and looks about.*)
MARY'S VOICE: Willie! Willie!
JOSEPH: (*loudly*) That is a very loud voice. What kind of voice is that?
(*Silence*)
(*Mary emerges from the sound booth rather hurriedly, picks up her mop and continues working.*)
MARY: It's nobody. Excuse me, I mean, it's only me; my name's Mary.
JOSEPH: You know, you could hear that all over the store.
MARY: You must've been mistaken.
JOSEPH: There's nothing wrong with my hearing—it's better than a lotta other people my age. Are you working tonight?
MARY: Temporary help.
(*Joseph, somewhat embarrassed, stands there. Silence. Mary continues her work.*)
JOSEPH: Well, I'll be going then. Good night.
MARY: Good night.
JOSEPH: Lemme ask you a question. Will you be here the whole night?
MARY: Oh no, my son and daughter-in-law are already waiting for me.
JOSEPH: Oh, so you're spending what they call Christmas eve with your loved ones, eh? As far as that kind of thing goes, I'm what you might call a "free thinker"—at least since 1928.
MARY: My daughter-in-law is making fish tonight and if I come too late . . . well, she won't be too pleased.
(*Silence. Mary works.*)
JOSEPH: Yes, since 1928 . . . I was a glass cutter at Goerz' Optical then . . . in the tenth district, and Tony Sedlacek, a friend and comrade, started off the whole thing . . . "Joseph," he said, "you know the whole idea of Christ is very unhistorical. You can't find anything about him in history—there's

nothing, absolutely nothing written, no sketches, no portraits, no sculptures, no etchings . . ."
(Silence. Mary looks over to Joseph.)

MARY: She gets the fish from the shop; well, the shop really belongs to him, but for tax purposes they say it belongs to her.

JOSEPH: If you're interested, I can tell you more. All known historians of the time—Roman as well as Jewish—have nothing to say about him. Flavius? Cornelius? Livy? Tacitus? Not a word. And he never wrote anything about himself either. So no one else writes anything about him. *(He laughs.)* The whole idea of God is nothing more than spiritual crutches for spiritual cripples.
(Mary turns away and continues her work. Joseph stands, quietly watching. Mary rinses out the mop. Joseph goes over to her quickly, takes the mop from her, and rinses it out himself.)

JOSEPH: If you don't mind . . . I hope I'm not bothering you.

MARY: I'm almost finished.
(Mary continues to work; Joseph follows her a bit, looking around the sales floor.)

JOSEPH: So full and yet so empty.
(Joseph trips over the brandy that Mary had placed beside the display shelves. He picks up the bottle, looks at it, then gazes off into the distance.)

JOSEPH: Demon alcohol. I know you well. My foster-father was a butcher, then he ran the welfare office in my town. He always felt good handwriting was very important. 1914—the beginning of the Great Slaughter—that's when he began to hit the bottle. He couldn't be drafted, he got out of it somehow. Hardly a Sunday went by when there wasn't a bottle of beer on the table. Then from beer he moved to wine, from wine to rum. The beginning of the month was always horrible, too. He'd come home at midnight, drunk as can be, and beat up my mother . . . my foster-mother. I'd run to the police. "What does your father do?" they'd ask me. "A civil servant? Well, go on home, it can't be all that bad," they'd say. And they sent me home.
(Joseph places the bottle back on the shelf. Mary goes over to him, takes the bottle from the shelf and places it back on the floor.)

MARY: I don't mean to interrupt . . . once in awhile I take a sip . . . to fight loneliness. But everything in moderation I always say.
(Joseph picks up the bottle.)
JOSEPH: I got an award from the Temperance League—and one from the Elks and from the Socialists as well. I was involved in politics a lot back then—with all my heart and soul. It turned me into an atheist. I mean, God, which can't exist, which couldn't exist, God won't be too sorry not to get my money.
(Joseph places the bottle on the shelf again. Mary takes the bottle, placing it beside the shelves a second time. Joseph picks up the bottle again.)
JOSEPH: On February 13, 1934 I was a guest in Commissary Fifteen when the commissar took off my temperance medal . . . I screamed at the damned fascists, "Is it a crime to be against alcohol?" You see, I had him beat—because of my background in the theater.
(Joseph places the bottle on the shelf. Mary takes it and places it beside the shelf.)
JOSEPH: *(looks at Mary)* Was no good to me then, really, my background in the theater, he hit me anyway . . . because of the noise I made.
MARY: *(looks at Joseph)* A person is just too good for this life. Too good even for your own children. Sometimes I think it's better you just go . . . that you just go away. People don't worry about you, it's the truth, I'm tellin' it like it is.
(Mary puts the bottle away; she continues her work. Joseph quickly opens his pocket and pulls out a newspaper, **The Truth.** *He follows her as she works.)*
JOSEPH: You know, not enough people subscribe to this paper. Why is that, I wonder? Is it because people are just too stupid? Or is it the unholy effect of Capitalism? Probably both. Sometimes I dream—free-thinkers don't dream much, but when they do, look out! Sometimes I dream that everyone wants a copy of this paper. Doors and windows all over the projects fly open and everybody wants a copy of **The Truth.** And I tell everyone not to push, there's enough for all. And in a second I've filled my subscription quota.
(Mary works on; Joseph holds a copy of **The Truth** *in front*

of her face.)

JOSEPH: The first three months are cheap.

MARY: I don't want to interrupt . . . in the women's pages an eighty-seven year old woman wrote in who says she goes hungry everyday because her son and daughter-in-law never make her meals.

JOSEPH: Two-thirds of humanity goes hungry every night—and you can read about that in these pages. You can get a trial subscription.

MARY: Dr. Schoeller, he writes the advice column, he wrote back and said that she had to be more assertive or else she should go into an old-age home.

(*Joseph opens* **The Truth**—*he puts on his reading glasses.*)

JOSEPH: A sampling from our talented poet, comrade Fritz Landl —murdered by Nazi thugs in Stein: Silent night, Holy Night/ I am hungry and cold and kept well in sight/ Alone in my cell I muse/ Thinking of love and the life we choose./ I think back on my days from youth to man/ It's true, mankind, our lot is tough/ A life of sorrow and if that's not enough/ A sea of pain our dreams destroy/ Hope robs us and so does Joy./ Yet I won't waste the days/ They strengthen us, our will obeys./ Today is Christmas for every bloke/ A day of love— it seems such a joke./ Where then is love, where indeed/ The tale of the burgeoning seed./ Silent the night, holy the night/ I am hungry, I'm cold and kept well in sight./ I think full of yearning of those I hold dear/ Think of the future and the coming new year . . . You know, he had polio and it crippled his right hand; so he wrote that poem with his left hand . . . on Christmas eve, 1940.

MARY: I don't mean to interrupt . . .

(*Drying her hands on her smock, Mary digs into her pocket and pulls out a newspaper clipping.*)

MARY: (*reading*) "I would like to pour out my heart although no one can help me. My daughter-in-law locks the groceries away from me. I am not allowed to eat anything and am always hungry. More often than not my friends must buy me coffee when we go out to a cafe. *She* receives my pension. I am eighty-seven years old. Do I deserve such treatment in my old age?" That's life for you.

(*Mary crams the clipping back into her pocketbook and*

continues her work. Joseph folds **The Truth** *back into his pocket. He watches her. He takes the rags from her, rinses them out.*)

MARY: Is your family waiting?

JOSEPH: I was given over to the orphanage in Margareten with the stipulation that I belong to whomever would have me. Some people did come, as a matter of fact, named Datschke from around Breslau somewhere. They later became my foster-parents. Legally my mother could have visited me, too, but only as an aunt or something.

MARY: My son is a nice boy, but he's too good to her. He is big-boned and likes to lie in bed all the time. She screams at him—"Not on the bed, I just made it!" "Put your feet on the footstool!" she says. It breaks my heart to hear that. So I give him fresh-baked bread. And she grabs it away because of the crumbs, she says. You've never seen such a hateful woman in all your life.

(*Mary looks at Joseph.*)

MARY: I bet your wife is an angel compared to her.

JOSEPH: Dr. Friedmann—he was a Tolstoyan—he held lectures at the night school in Ottakring about sexuality, you know, sex and hygiene. He talked a little about dating but kept everything pretty much clinical. In 1939, he had to leave; he settled down somewhere between Detroit and Chicago . . . Around Christmas, '46, I got a letter from him. I've even memorized some of it. "My son"—that's what he called me, I was a lot younger then, makes sense, I guess. "Your love belongs to the exploited and betrayed masses . . ."

MARY: I don't mean to interrupt . . . They're probably sitting down together now. Her cooking is always much too spicy.

(*Silence. Mary works.*)

JOSEPH: Then you'll have to be going soon, I imagine.

(*Silence. Mary cleans the floor, machinelike. The same small section, over and over.*)

JOSEPH: It's been nice talking to you. Sorry you gotta go.

(*Silence. Mary cleans. Suddenly, she drops her mop and leaves. Joseph goes after her.*)

MARY: He has gallstones, but you wouldn't think so when you see what she fixes for him. So I bring him food at work— without telling her. She never telephones when something's wrong with him.

(*Mary takes two glasses from a display. She goes over to the brandy, which still stands beside the shelves. Joseph follows her.*)

MARY: Still, I'm bringing her perfume—the most expensive I can find—and him a sweater and my grandson a train. They'll get my presents even if I have to leave it on the steps outside.

(*Mary takes the brandy and goes to the couch. Joseph follows.*)

MARY: I'm just an ordinary cleaning woman. I've even gotten a freezer so that when he comes to visit I have something in the house for him to eat. And here I am giving her the most expensive perfume . . . I have to, or else he catches hell.

(*Mary sits on the couch, opens the bottle of brandy, pours herself a glass, then raises it up. Joseph, horrified by this, watches.*)

MARY: Little Miss Mary—brave, clean and reverent. You can even leave your wallet with me—nothing will happen to it . . . but if anything happens to him, little Miss Mary won't be so brave and clean—watch out. Then people will stand up and take notice.

(*Mary empties the glass in one gulp.*)

JOSEPH: No more Mr. Nice Guy, eh?

(*Mary pours herself a second glass; she holds it out for Joseph.*)

JOSEPH: No. No. You can't catch an old Injun that easily! My name is Thomas—today the die is cast—Today the chapter on Louis Capet reaches its dramatic climax . . . I was an extra at the theater in Graz, you know. I got the part from the great actor, Karl Drews—he was killed by the Nazis.

(*Mary holds the glass out to him.*)

MARY: The Rock of Gibraltar, Dakar, Senegal, Portugal, Lisbon— that's me all right.

(*Mary continues to hold the glass out to him; she looks imploringly at Joseph.*)

MARY: Please, sir.

JOSEPH: You've got to realize that my foster-parents used to give me alcohol whenever I cried.

MARY: Please, if you don't want to believe.

(*Mary puts the glass down; takes a photograph from her wallet and holds it out to Joseph. Joseph sits down on the*

Joseph and Mary 65

couch, takes his reading glasses out of his pocket, puts them on. The photograph is faded with age; Joseph looks at it closely. Mary pulls her dress up over her knees and looks at Joseph.)
MARY: Now you know everything.
JOSEPH: (*without looking up*) I see a scantily clad woman and a zebra.
MARY: I'm the zebra. It was a variety show in Lisbon . . . 1932. That's my partner next to me. She was luckier—a diplomat took an interest in her. She left the profession and went straight into an elegant apartment. She did have a touch of tuberculosis and looked a bit ragged now and then. About 1955 or '56, I'm not sure anymore exactly, I ran into her on the Boulevard . . . I'm sure she's dead by now.
(*Mary drinks.*)
MARY: For forty years I've acted as if I was never in show business. Sometimes, it's been pretty hard to do. And when I worked at Kapp's, you know, the radio store, and did more than my share, the boss was very nice and when my colleagues said they'd hit me if I raised up the quota too high, I thought to myself, what d'you know. And a few days ago, when my daughter-in-law stood behind my son and my son said, "Mama, please don't come by on Christmas eve or there'll be problems," then I thought to myself, that fresh, awful face of hers and I thought to myself, "you were never in show business, you were never on stage."
(*Mary shakes her head repeatedly.*)
MARY: You can kill an old lady, but you can't do in an artist.
(*Mary holds her bared leg out to Joseph. Joseph regards her leg.*)
MARY: That's the leg of a ballerina. Still firm.
(*Mary moves to take Joseph's hand to her leg; he pulls his hand away. He puts on his reading glasses and searches in his pocket.*)
JOSEPH: If I may bring a letter to your attention. the last letter of one of our comrades . . . first at the Commissary, then the hospital outpost, then the detention headquarters on Hermann Street, then the Courthouse . . . then, they killed him. They cut off his head . . . . "My dear wife, Fate has determined that I must end my young life. I have just been informed that

my appeal for mercy has been denied. Now it is inevitable. I depart this life with a clear conscience and prepared, for I know I have done nothing wrong. For that which I have done I am not ashamed. I gave my all in duty to humanity. All for the cause of the exploited masses. I hope, too, that you are not ashamed to have had a husband who cared for the oppressed and who presented these feelings openly and honestly. I apologize for the worry and sorrow I have caused you. Do not bear it heavily. It has not been in vain. For the last time, receive my sincere appreciation for everything. Life with you has been beautiful."

(*While he reads, Joseph becomes increasingly excited. He trembles. Mary holds the full glass of brandy out to him.*)

JOSEPH: "This has given me strength to bear my fate for these seventeen long months. Everything which belongs to me or has belonged to me is now yours. Unfortunately, I could not acquire more. I hope my last wish to have my body released to you will be honored. Bury me where you please—it is all the same to me. I do ask you not to become discouraged; there is no use for that. Think, rather, I have given my life for the oppressed of the world . . . ."

(*Joseph trembles over his whole body. Mary tries to force the brandy down his throat; Joseph backs away.*)

MARY: Don't turn away when you're in this condition.

JOSEPH: "Go proudly as if I were coming home one day. Begin a new life as you should and that is worthy of you. I wish you much luck and fine friends. Give my love once again to all our friends . . . all dear people"—he had to write "friends" because the word "comrade" was forbidden, of course. "Be true to the mountains and to nature. Greet them for me—I will always be with you. Do not cry, but begin again anew. Be strong in spite of everything. Much love and kisses from your dearly loving . . . Joseph."

(*Joseph is totally beside himself. Again, Mary tries with the brandy. Joseph turns away.*

JOSEPH: (*cries out*) The walls must be high everywhere! They have to build walls, walls against their fascist barbarism!!

(*Joseph buries his head in his hands. Silence. Mary places her hands on his head.*)

MARY: I don't mean to interrupt but . . . an old man really

doesn't have much to laugh about. That's the truth, I'm just tellin' it like it is.
(Joseph sits up with a jerk. He searches wildly for his identification card, finally holding it in front of Mary.)
JOSEPH: There, look—the signature: Joseph Pribil.
(Joseph holds the ID card next to the letter.)
JOSEPH: The same as on the letter.
(Silence)
MARY: Oh, so you wrote the letter?
(Silence. Joseph nods.)
MARY: To your dear wife. So you do have a wife.
(Joseph looks at Mary; Mary looks at Joseph. Joseph takes a glass of brandy, downing it in one swallow.)
JOSEPH: She is not here.
MARY: Died so young?
JOSEPH: *(cries out)* As if she ever lived!!
(Silence)
MARY: Oh, so you wrote the letter to a wife who never lived? My husband was in the Quartermaster Corps in Narvik. You're really very lonely, too.
JOSEPH: A progressive man is never alone. At the World's Fair for Youth in 1959 there were twenty thousand young people.
(Mary refills his glass.)
MARY: They don't like us much, young people, I mean. I come into the fish store with some food for my son—sometimes he's not there, only her and the customers. So she says to one of them, and loud enough for me to hear: "That's the old lady, there." If I say something about it, my son catches hell. So I pick up my things, clean up and all the time I can feel everybody looking at me.
(The two click glasses and drink.)
MARY: Joseph, if I may call you that, today is Christmas.
(Joseph smiles.)
JOSEPH: I signed on for extra work—it's over quicker that way.
MARY: Joseph, I think God sent you here. Oh, if my husband were still alive . . . In those days I had to leave Lisbon and return immediately to Germany. You know— Hitler called on all artists to come home.
JOSEPH: The Fiver, Adolf Killer, the hysterical Bozo: Mr. Schickelgruber. The hired assassin of Capitalism.

MARY: We had a squad leader in the League of German Maidens who broiled a whole goose with the insides still in the goose—it made no sense at all. Frau Stadler went to Berchtesgaden with her "Strength through Joy" group. She saw the Führer and said we just couldn't imagine how it was; the man was a god. I was at an airbase in Auffing in Bavaria—at the laundry—and one day he came in all decked out in a brilliant uniform . . . my future husband, that is.

JOSEPH: I'm starting to feel a little strange.

(*Joseph laughs.*)

MARY: He wanted me to iron some pants for him. Joseph, do you know how often he used to come in?

(*Joseph laughs.*)

MARY: Three times a day. They didn't have the pill in those days and when he had to go with the Corps to Narvik, I was already pregnant.

(*Joseph drinks and giggles.*)

JOSEPH: When I want to, I can be Teresa of Konnersreuth. I can suck on my gums until they start to bleed. That saved me. And then I acted like an epileptic. So I made it through. I'm the only comrade who made it.

MARY: Arms and legs froze up—up there. It was practical for us, though, because we would get blood sausage and bacon more easily. But he never forgave me for that business with the Czech . . . not even on his death-bed. And we really didn't do anything. I just wanted to learn a bit of the language because, well, his folks were Czech and I wanted to be able to talk to them when he introduced me.

JOSEPH: When they were going to take me away I made up my mind I wasn't me, I was someone else. And I had to be that person completely. I can still hear the steps of those brown-shirted thugs in the hallway. How they threw open the door . . I stared them down—blood ran down from the corners of my mouth. Yessir, gentlemen, you can't catch an Indian that easily. My name is Thomas—and today the die is cast; today the chapter on Louis Capet comes to an end. Like I said, it was all an act—and an epileptic to boot. They brought me to the psycho ward. They called it the upside-down ward. A guy called Dr. Lorenzoni examined me. Let them beat me up, he said. I should admit that I was faking, he said. Uh-uh, gentlemen, you can't catch an Indian that easily. You know, I could've had a career as an actor if Reyer hadn't wrecked it.

MARY: The baby came and my husband was off at war. The child never knew the things I had to go through. In 1945 I went all the way from Bavaria to Vienna with my baby; first in a pushcart, then an oxcart. On foot, nothing to eat: I was sick and when I got to Vienna, my in-laws' house, there was my husband, out back with the boys, playing cards.

JOSEPH: Reyer wanted to give out autographs, but didn't have any paper. I was standing behind him. I was already an extra at the Burgtheater, so I handed him a piece of paper: he signed it, turned it over and read the other side: "Down with the exploiting classes! Long live international solidarity! Down with warmongering and profiteering!" I was fired, even though I was doing pretty well—in 1928 I was in Fritz Lang's production of *Sodom and Gomorrah* in Laaerberg.

(*Mary refills his glass; Joseph and Mary continue to drink.*)

MARY: My husband used to hit me a lot. Especially when we talked about this business with the Czech fellow. Joseph, you're a good man. I have just one child, my son, Willie.

JOSEPH: And ever since then, I've dedicated myself to the Party. It's all very interesting.

MARY: Why are people so awful? Joseph, tell me that.

JOSEPH: People and humanity . . . long live the progressive masses! And there are a lot of them, you know. And their numbers are growing and growing. I'm just one of them. Just the tip of the iceberg . . .

MARY: Why would my son say that he wants to lead his own life? Without my help? So who's stopping him? I'm still his mother. Joseph, you know I once was a beautiful woman.

JOSEPH: My real mother never visited me . . . She was in the theater, too. A colleague of mine, a guy called Gundolf Auer, told me once that a Hungarian film reminded him a lot of the life my mother led. It was called *Mrs. Dery*. I've looked for it at movie theaters ever since, but I never have found it.

MARY: A man came into my mother's grocery store and gave me a ticket. He expected me to come that evening to his box at the opera. He told me that all the way from Constantinople. . .

JOSEPH: The world turns, Copernicus was right, the world turns.
MARY: Take a look at this . . . that's the picture from the Variety—at home I have a whole shoe-box full of photographs from those days. You know, Joseph, I used to be really quite beautiful.
(Mary closes her eyes and moves her face close to Joseph's.)
MARY: My name was Mia Ritter—I changed it from Maria Patzak.
(Joseph stands up abruptly. He totters toward the shelves, takes a package of bread off the shelf.)
JOSEPH: How much is this bread? Shameful! In 1945 bread cost twenty-five cents a loaf; then it went to sixty cents, then a dollar eighteen, then a dollar-ninety, two-seventy, three-sixty and on, on and so on . . . Did wages go up that fast? It all started with this demonic wage-price agreement—or maybe with the streetcar ride for twenty-five cents . . .
(Joseph totters back and forth. Several items topple off the shelves; Mary goes over to him and holds him up.)
MARY: C'mon, Joseph—Let's treat ourselves.
(Mary drags him through the sales floor toward the sound booth. Joseph stops frequently, swaying back and forth.)
JOSEPH: And today it costs a dollar. That's four times what it was in forty-five. Have the wages of the working man gone up that fast? A salad used to cost seven cents, an egg nine or ten cents—depending on the size. Good chocolate was ten cents, too. And I always hesitated to buy it, it seemed so expensive. Welfare checks got up to nine-fifty—so help me, it's the truth.
(Joseph's voice becomes gradually louder, more strident.)
JOSEPH: And meat! Meat. I used to eat meat once a year on Good Friday. That's because I was such a free-thinker, back then. Otherwise, potatoes, tripe, cow udders and stuff like that— that's what I ate. No one remembers those days now, it's all forgotten. Now I drive from Purkersdorf to Liesing, from Schwechat to Grossenzerdorf so that I can save a few cents on milk. For example—at Konsum's—and I'm not trying to plug brands, you know—bread costs eighty-nine cents, I go over to Hofer—there they have it on sale for eighty. There are still people around like us—all you have to do is listen to the Caritas Charity announcements on the radio. Why all this when we live in a prosperous country like this place,

huh? And how many hundreds of thousands of workers are there out there—I'm not talking about skilled ones, just unskilled ones, who only earn four hundred, maybe five hundred dollars a month? And I'm not even talking about the women! The maids or migrants or old women on fixed pensions. But just you wait—you can't catch an old Indian that easily. My name is Thomas. Today the die is cast.
(*Mary disappears with Joseph behind the door of the sound booth. Silence. Static is heard over the PA system.*)
MARY'S VOICE: You have to push this button—then it'll work.
(*Silence*)
MARY'S VOICE: Say something, Joseph.
(*Silence*)
JOSEPH'S VOICE: Dr. Lorenzoni who let them beat me up lives in Graz now.
MARY'S VOICE: Whatever you want, no one can hear us.
JOSEPH'S VOICE: On his door on Marian Street you can see his nameplate: "Dr. Egon Lorenzoni, MD—Neurologist." and then, under that: "Dr. Peter Lorenzoni, MD" That's probably his son.
MARY'S VOICE: It doesn't matter—whatever you can think of . . .
JOSEPH'S VOICE: You know, Mary, sometimes I go to his house and stand under his window and just look up.
MARY'S VOICE: Here, you have to speak into the microphone.
JOSEPH'S VOICE: Peoples of the world, heed our call—onward for the final campaign! The International fights for human dignity!
MARY'S VOICE: You can talk or sing . . . no one's listening. The store is empty. If I say "Willie" it doesn't matter, he can't hear it.
(*Silence*)
MARY'S VOICE: Willie, are you thinking of your mother on Christmas?
JOSEPH'S VOICE: Silent night, holy night. On Christmas eve, 1936, Franco bombed Madrid. Nixon celebrated the same way in Hanoi in 1972. Christmas eve. Murderers!
(*Silence.*)
MARY'S VOICE: Merry Christmas. It sounds loud, but no one can hear.
(*Silence*)

JOSEPH'S VOICE: Mary?
MARY'S VOICE: Yes, Joseph?
JOSEPH'S VOICE: I heard you. From the very first word.
(*Silence*)
MARY'S VOICE: But you didn't see me when I looked very elegant.
(*Silence*)
JOSEPH'S VOICE: What are you doing? I don't feel so good. I have to sit down.
(*Silence. Static is heard from the PA system. Joseph and Mary come out of the sound booth. Mary is no longer wearing her bandana. Joseph goes to the couch, sits down and gazes off into space. Mary picks up the store items which had fallen during Joseph's spell of tottering. She rearranges the items back on the shelf. She goes to Joseph. She puts the top back on the brandy, and wipes the glasses clean with a towel. Silence.*)
JOSEPH: (*still staring off into space*) Otto's buried in a graveyard in Neustift. Fritz was executed in Stein. Hans is dead, Arthur, too, and no word from Professor Fried since the postcard in February, 1953. I'm the last comrade.
MARY: When my neighbor died, they put her things out on the sidewalk. I looked to see if there was anything I could use. There were old report cards from elementary school, some good grades, too. Letters from her husband from the first World War. There was nothing interesting in them, just love stuff. The next day the garbage men took it all away. What's left of you when there's nothing left of you? I'll tell you— it's just better to go when you can . . .
JOSEPH: In order to give my insanity a touch of authenticity, it was necessary that I had to try and hang myself. I climbed up on the stove, the burner was still a bit warm, and I put the noose around my neck. Then I waited for the guard. I had to wait awhile and while I was waiting, I looked through the top window. I could see the park and a girl in a white dress. Suddenly the guard screamed at me, "Are you crazy!" he said. And you know, I couldn't think of anything to say to him.
(*Mary takes up her mop, bucket and wet rags; she goes behind the stage. Joseph stares out into space. Silence. Mary returns with the wastepaper basket. She places the basket on the*

couch and looks at Joseph.)
MARY: Well, it's about that time.
(*Joseph looks at Mary.*)
JOSEPH: Mary, you have been given a peek into the world political situation as it is today. What do you think, will we live to see the victory of real socialism?
MARY: Things are so different in the world these days . . . much colder.
(*Mary sits down next to Joseph.*)
MARY: Who cares about us? Who touches our lives?
(*Mary smoothes her wrinkled skin on her hand, and holds it out toward Joseph.*)
MARY: Who would want to touch a thing like that?
(*Joseph pulls out his glasses, puts them on and looks closely at Mary's outstretched hand.*)
JOSEPH: When I was a glass cutter at Goerz' Optical, I had to breathe in glass dust all the time. Then they threw me out and wrote in my file: "healthy and salary paid up in full." But I used to cough up blood all the time.
(*Joseph opens his uniform shirt and unbuttons a few buttons of his old-fashioned undershirt. He takes his finger and pushes down on his chest.*)
JOSEPH: I was in the sanitarium at Enzenback six times. That's where I was fitted with a Pneumothorax. You know, it pulls air up between the pleura and air sacs.
(*Joseph takes a deep breath in and out, still pressing down on his chest.*)
JOSEPH: Today I'm negative, completely negative.
(*Mary raises up her smock and slip and holds her half-exposed back out to Joseph.*)
MARY: Right next to the spinal column . . . you have to press down to tell . . . that's where I have pain from a disc. I've been to the waters at Bad Tatzmannsdorf three times, and still the pain won't go away.
(*Joseph looks at her back and then at his fingers. He wiggles his fingers.*)
JOSEPH: I have some circulation problems in my fingers . . .
MARY: You have to press, otherwise I don't feel the pain.
(*Joseph taps his index finger lightly on her back.*)
JOSEPH: Done.

MARY: That was no pressing—not for my money.
(*Joseph presses again.*)
MARY: Harder. More to the right. Still harder. There it is, there's the pain. If you don't have any discs out of whack, you just can't imagine the pain.
(*Joseph holds up a part of his coat and shirt so that some of his chest is exposed.*)
JOSEPH: I did cough once—one time, in the opera—during my second try at a career.
(*Mary presses her finger on Joseph's breast-bone. Joseph breathes in and out deeply. Mary's pressing quickly changes into caressing.*)
JOSEPH: They promised me the role of a lion in *The Magic Flute*. The director taught me to growl real loud. Sure, the part was pretty easy: they gave me a lion costume and put the head on—the only problem was that I never thought that the head would be filled with dust inside. And so, when I was supposed to growl, all I could do was start coughing. They couldn't use a coughing lion in *The Magic Flute*.
MARY: Sure, because of the music . . .
JOSEPH: Maria Cebotari, a wonderful singer—had cancer. Oeggl something, I've forgotten his last name, baritone. Rucicka, she was a Yugoslav. Otto Langer, Jan Kiepura with his wife Martha Eggert and Helga Roswaenge in *La Bohème*!. .
MARY: I only went to the opera once—with the gentleman who wanted to send me to Constantinople. I always thought God would protect me, you know. But when that man made his advances in the box at the opera, well, I thought to myself, "thy will be done." You're only young and dumb once, you know.
JOSEPH: Well, listen, I'm not much of a poet, but I have written some things down. And how do I live? Well, I get along. A lot of wonderful tunes have come out of this throat. As an extra you're always hanging around, and you know you tend to pick things up. I really could've played all of the big roles, you know.
MARY: Carlos Gardel.
JOSEPH: Who?
MARY: Carlos Gardel. Every kid in Casablanca knows that name. A tango singer. Do you tango, Joseph?

JOSEPH: Since my foster-father spent every dime he had on booze, there was hardly enough for dance lessons . . .
MARY: It's real easy—just look at my legs . . .
(Mary stands and does a few tango steps for Joseph)
MARY: Look, Joseph. One and two and tango—and one and two and tango. When I say "and" dip with me. Wait, I'll put on some music and it'll be easier.
*(Mary goes to the record section, selects a record. Joseph buttons up his shirt and tunic as quickly as he can; puts on his glasses, takes out **The Truth** from his pocket and begins reading intently. Mary puts on a tango record; she turns the volume up quite loud, then returns to Joseph.)*
MARY: Joseph, let's tango!
JOSEPH: This is a very interesting article, if you'll just let me read you a little . . . "In the Soviet Union grain production is up over 30% in the last ten years. Soybeans on the other hand . . ."
MARY: C'mon Joseph—tonight the die is cast—you said so yourself.
(Mary pulls him up, holds him tightly and drags him across the stage.)
MARY: It's really easy, you know. One and two and tango, one and two and tango. Now, hold me around the waist, tightly, I bend back and you bend forward . . . over me, like this.
JOSEPH: Excuse me, I can't.
MARY: Of course you can. Bend forward, not backward. Forward. One and two and tango . . .
JOSEPH: When I was young enough for this kind of thing, naturally, I took some lessons at the Union Hall on Mollard Street. Physics, too. I was really interested in that as well. Speed of light—all that stuff . . . I used to get up at five o'clock in the morning, my room wasn't heated, then I'd go to the factory to work, then study until two in the morning. Latin vocabulary, Austria under the Romans, and so forth. I had to realize that life went on without a diploma, without Latin or the Punic Wars. Life had to go on.
MARY: C'mon, you've almost got it—one and two and tango. You have a natural talent for it.
JOSEPH: Me?
MARY: Sure, listen, I know who can dance and who can't.

JOSEPH: And you think I can dance?
MARY: Don't forget, keep bending over . . .
(*Joseph bends deeply over her.*)
MARY: Look at how you do that; it's so elegant.
(*The two tango. Joseph is totally transformed. He has taken over the part of the lead. The record comes to an end. Joseph lets go of Mary, moves to the record player and begins the record again. He returns to Mary and grasps her around the waist.*)
JOSEPH: Mary, let's tango!
(*The two dance an even quicker paced tango.*)
MARY: (*laughing*) Joseph, I don't recognize you . . .
JOSEPH: (*loudly*) No one knows me. For years, oh hell, for my whole life I've been some kind of outsider, always second string. (*he laughs*) But tonight! The die has been cast . . .
(*Joseph pulls Mary closer and dances wildly.*)
MARY: Why, Joseph! This is like dancing with Rudolph Valentino!
JOSEPH: And who was that gentleman?
MARY: The Sheik—King of the Desert, the Hero of the New World. He was always well-groomed, a very nice looking man. He combed his hair straight back.
(*Joseph lets go of Mary, looks around, takes a bottle of mineral water from the display shelves, pours some onto his hands, rubs the water onto his hair and, with a somewhat gap-toothed comb, combs his hair straight back. Mary looks at him and laughs. Joseph takes her around the waist and regards her voluptuously.*)
JOSEPH: Like this?
MARY: (*laughing*) You're a character.
JOSEPH: I am Valentine, or whatever his name was. Now can't you tell I was in the theater?
MARY: Valentin-o. Rudolph Valentino. He was the most elegant man of the Age. Always wore a tuxedo, even in the desert.
JOSEPH: Your wish is my command . . .
(*Joseph lets go of Mary, runs to the clothing section. He rummages around, pulls out a tuxedo, takes off his security guard uniform and replaces it with the tuxedo jacket, which is at least one size too large. He runs back to Mary.*)
JOSEPH: (*loudly*) Tango!
(*Joseph takes Mary firmly around the waist. The record is*

over, Joseph scurries over to the record player.)
JOSEPH: (*laughing*) Not so fast, gentlemen. You can't catch an old Indian that easily.
(*Joseph starts the record again. He takes Mary, they dance the tango at a wilder pace than ever before.*)
JOSEPH: Am I Valentino or am I not Valentino?
MARY: (*laughing*) One thing's missing, Joseph.
JOSEPH: Tell me what it is, I can act out anything.
MARY: (*laughing*) He seduced women by the dozen. No one could resist his advances . . .
JOSEPH: (*laughing*) Will you be able to resist me when I make an offer you can't refuse?
(*Mary laughs.*)
JOSEPH: Yes or no!?
(*Silence. Joseph and Mary continue to dance. Suddenly, Mary releases Joseph and looks at him intently.*)
MARY: (*seriously, with a touch of tragic resignation*) Yes, I won't be able to resist you, Joseph.
(*Joseph stares at her. Mary moves resolutely to a large bed display and pulls back the covers. Joseph takes off his glasses, cleans them and puts them back on. The record is over. Silence. Mary unbuttons her smock. Joseph regards her, not quite comprehending. Suddenly, Mary stops and smiles at Joseph.*)
MARY: Don't you think it's just a little too bright in here, Joseph? Would you mind dimming the lights?
JOSEPH: Yes, of course. I know just where the lights are, too. It's my job, you know.
(*Joseph goes behind the stage—or into a corner of the stage—to a visible or assumed switchbox. Total darkness. Joseph returns to the darkened stage. He taps about in the darkness. Display goods are heard crashing onto the floor.*)
MARY: (*calling out*) It's okay.
(*Joseph wanders about in the dark.*)
JOSEPH: No, it's too risky.
(*Joseph goes back to the "switchbox." Light again. He goes back to Mary. She lies in bed, holding the cover just over her breasts. She smiles.*)
MARY: Just like in the soap operas—Mia Ritter—Queen of the Oriental Ballet.

(*Mary laughs and wiggles her feet underneath the covers.*)
JOSEPH: Those things aren't good for you.
(*While Joseph talks, he removes his tuxedo jacket and returns it to its place in the clothing section. He places his guard tunic neatly beside the bed. As well as his shoes, shirt and long-sleeved underwear.*)
JOSEPH: Millions of people watch that stuff and it addles their brains, even of the smartest person. And when you think how much statistics tell us a person watches in a day—whew! And what's the result of it all? People stop reading things like *The Truth*. Subscriptions go way down and no one renews.
(*Joseph is finished undressing. He is wearing only briefs, socks and garters. He climbs into bed, as if it were a matter of going to bed like any other night. Three feet separate him from Mary. Both Joseph and Mary have pulled up the covers to their chins, and look straight ahead. Silence. Mary moves closer. She lays her head on Joseph's shoulder.*)
JOSEPH: Mary?
MARY: Yes, Joseph?
JOSEPH: I guess this situation requires more than mere friendship.
(*Mary looks earnestly at Joseph.*)
MARY: My name is Mary. (*Joseph shakes her hand.*)
JOSEPH: And I am Joseph . . . hold on. (*Joseph jumps out of bed.*)
MARY: What are you going to do now?
(*Joseph takes the brandy and two fresh glasses off the shelves. He returns to bed. He fills the glasses, gives one to Mary and raises his in a toast. Joseph stands in briefs, socks and garters, raising his glass toward Mary.*)
JOSEPH: My dearest Mary, there are moments in the lives of two people when the level of attraction reaches a certain fever pitch and sex is only a matter of time. We don't need priests or marriage ceremonies. We don't need the ritual of the thing; we want to enter into this, the most beautiful experience one person can give to another, with open eyes and a clear understanding. So, I propose a toast—to our new-found love.
(*Joseph drinks his brandy in one swallow.*)
MARY: No, not like that. We have to drink together.
JOSEPH: Oh, excuse me.
(*Joseph fills his glass again. The two drink, this time their*

arms are entwined. The glasses are empty. Mary closes her eyes, and holds her face up to Joseph's. Joseph refills his glass and gazes at Mary.)
MARY: (*her eyes still closed*) Before I had even been kissed by any man, I was all excited about the prospect of it . . . about the kiss that seals love.
(*Joseph kisses Mary. He holds his glass clumsily so that the brandy spills onto the bed. Mary draws away from him.*)
MARY: That's funny, all of a sudden it feels wet here.
(*Mary sees what has happened. She climbs out of bed: she is still dressed in her work clothes.*)
MARY: Oh God, the sheets!
(*Joseph sees the wet spot on the sheets; he takes a swig directly from the bottle.*)
JOSEPH: Excuse me, I'm terribly sorry, you big bosses of this department store. You guys who feed on our money; who suck it out of us . . . I'm terribly sorry that we've spilled brandy on your valuable sheets. But now is the moment of truth. Tonight the die is cast . . . That's it, period. I, Joseph Pribil, declare that this warehouse of capitalist greed has become the property of the people, and therefore, I order, get another set of sheets, Mary.
MARY: But, we have to pay for all this, Joseph.
JOSEPH: Pay? We don't have to pay a cent, Mary. We have lost our minds and are no longer responsible for our actions. During Party meetings it's always, "old Joseph." He can sell our papers for us, but don't allow him to take part in the discussions. He lost his mind long ago. And when young kids see me on the street with my garters and shorts, I hear what they say. They say, "Look at that crazy old geezer." They don't understand that socks without garters get caught in the bike chain. The fascists threw me in an insane asylum. I lost my rights. And, well, I'm the same way now. Mary, let's tango!
(*Joseph takes her around the waist and turns in a circle.*)
MARY: They always say that I'm nuts, too. So senile, they say I oughta lose my driver's license.
(*Joseph releases Mary; he goes to the shelves; with complete self-assuredness, he removes goods from the shelf. The goods he does not care for he shoves to one side or throws behind*

him. *Mary goes to the bedding section to get some new sheets.*)

JOSEPH: Asparagus, too much lead, unhealthy. Lox is better. Caviar, from Russia most likely. I'll have some of that in any case. Crackers . . . only makes you thirsty. Dried fruit dipped in chocolate . . . now, that sounds better.

(*Joseph becomes more confident and audacious. He examines each item, keeps it or casts it off according to his mood. Mary comes with fresh sheets and puts them on the bed. Joseph has his hands full of goods. He goes to Mary and lays the merchandise at her feet.*)

MARY: I knew a car dealer in Albania. He was generous, too. Joseph, wait a minute.

(*Mary goes to her paper shopping bag and brings forth the three packages wrapped as Christmas gifts. She places them before Joseph.*)

MARY: These belong to you.

(*Joseph looks at her.*)

MARY: Go ahead, open them.

(*Joseph opens the largest package first.*)

MARY: That was for my son.

(*Joseph opens the package to find a sweater; he puts it on. The sweater is several sizes too large. He opens the next package: a small bottle of perfume. Joseph opens the perfume and sprays a small bit under his shoulders and behind his ears. He opens the third package: a toy electric train. Joseph holds the locomotive in his hand and looks at Mary. He kneels before her.*)

JOSEPH: "My beloved wife . . . fate has decided that I must end my young life. Just now I have received word that my appeal for mercy has been denied. Now it is inevitable. I depart this life with a clear conscience and prepared, for I know I have done nothing wrong. For that which I have done I am not ashamed. I gave my all in duty to humanity. All for the cause of the exploited masses. I hope, too, that you are not ashamed to have had a husband who cared for the oppressed and who presented these feelings openly and honestly. I apologize for the worry and sorrow I have caused you. Do not bear it heavily. It has not been in vain. For the last time, receive my sincere appreciation for everything. Life with you

has been beautiful."
MARY: You really are nuts . . . but sure a great poet!
(*Mary takes his head and lays it in her lap. Joseph sobs. Mary brings him to bed, like a child. She lies next to him. Silence.*)
MARY: Are you ticklish, Joseph?
JOSEPH: Well, I don't know, I've never tickled myself.
(*Mary tickles him.*)
MARY: Is little Joey ticklish, is he, huh?
(*Joseph howls with laughter, he "snorts" and almost falls out of bed.*)
MARY: My God, you are ticklish, aren't you?
JOSEPH: Yes, very much.
(*Silence. The two move closer to one another. Mary lays her head under Joseph's arm.*)
MARY: My husband was so sick during those last years. Nothing like this was possible between us then. It's been ten years since he died. And, of course, there hasn't been anything since then, either. I think I've even forgotten how.
JOSEPH: My last time was on the train between Moscow and Leningrad . . . on the night of May 15, 1956. I had sold the most subscriptions for *The Truth* and had won a trip to the Soviet Union. I was in the sleeping car, in the berth above a very attractive comrade. Seeing as we had no religious restraints and it was the land of brotherly—and sisterly—love, they aren't as nervous about those things as we are . . . I went up to her under the cover of darkness. She threw an incredible fit, shouted at me—all in Russian. Well, you see not everything in socialism is cracked up as it's supposed to be. You have very nice skin, Mary.
(*Silence.*)
MARY: You should have known me forty-five years ago, Joseph.
JOSEPH: I was a starving, out-of-work worker then . . . sick with tuberculosis and always hanging around Party headquarters. You wouldn't have looked at me twice, Mary, no woman ever looked at me twice.
MARY: Let me think back . . . forty years. That was when I sent my mother a package from Casablanca. She refused to accept it because she said she wouldn't take anything from a daughter who walked around naked and let men look at her.
(*Silence.*)

MARY: Sometimes I wish I could start all over again. I wish life were still as white as new-fallen snow. Do you know that old game we used to play as children, Joseph?
JOSEPH: Yes. No, I mean, you know my rather tragic childhood.
MARY: We called it "Disappearing from the earth."
JOSEPH: How did it work?
MARY: Like this: you count to three. One . . . two . . . three . . .
JOSEPH: One . . . two . . . three . . .
MARY: You close your eyes tightly and hold your breath. Close 'em tight.
JOSEPH: They're closed.
(*Joseph and Mary have closed their eyes and hold hands.*)
JOSEPH: (*opening his eyes*) And what happens after you've opened your eyes again?
MARY: (*with closed eyes*) Whatever you've wished for comes true.
JOSEPH: I've had enough of that game.

END

A Social Engagement

Time of action: The present
Place: A villa in the wealthy suburbs

Dramatis Personae:

The family: Gustave Schneider, physician, 43
      Verena Schneider, his wife, 35
      Heiner Schneider, Gustave's son from his first marriage, 19
      The elder Schneider, 70
      Draga, the Yugoslav housekeeper
The guests: The writer, "permanent" guest, 37
      The theater producer, 45
      The theater producer's wife, 40
      The entrepreneur, 41
      The entrepreneur's wife, 46
      The member of Parliament, 44
      The actor (with a slight Italian accent), 38

The stage: The large living room in Gustave Schneider's villa. The back wall of the room is oval. Several windows and a door lead directly into the garden. At the audience's left is the small anteroom through which one enters the living room. At right, a free-standing stairway leads upstairs. Beneath the stairs one sees a small telephone table and a couch. A door into the kitchen is behind the stairs. Comfortable easy chairs, small side tables, a serving tray with drinks and a stereo stand in front of the window. In the foreground, left, there are several tables covered with white tablecloths. Tasteful flower arrangements decorate the table centers.

The music: The music should not only serve as a link between scenes, but also be heard during the scenes themselves. It should function as an integral part of the play's dramaturgy. To some extent the music should take on the characteristics of a film score.

The production: I implore directors of this play not to denunciate the characters here, let alone turn them into cabaret figures.

There are no "good" and "evil" characters here. All "badness" springs rather from a private bourgeois morality and its need for self-justification.

The language: The characters in this play have a disturbed relationship to language. Not they themselves, but their ability to interpret themselves and others is articulated. They are to a certain degree speechless. The decisive events occur not in the speaking, but in that realm beyond the spoken word.

Scene One

Late afternoon. Heiner Schneider, the Doctor's son, sits on the couch underneath the stairs—only the audience can see him. He is listening to a cassette recorder with earphones. In front of the window, through which one sees the garden, the writer sits in an easy chair, reading. In front of him, on a small table, several books lie next to another recorder. Next to him—the serving tray with drinks. Verena Schneider, the Doctor's wife, and Draga, the Yugoslav housekeeper, come out from the kitchen and carry cold-cut platters to the tables covered with white tablecloths. They go back to the kitchen and return with more trays. This action is repeated several times—there is going to be a rather extravagant selection of hors d'oeuvres.

Finally, the buffet table is ready. The housekeeper returns to the kitchen; Verena examines the table, straightening and ordering the arrangement as necessary.

VERENA: (*with a look to the Writer*) I regard myself as a socialist only in the sense that I think each individual has a right to develop himself and his talents as much as possible. You can use that for your play, can't you?
She goes to the Writer, runs her fingers through his hair, laughs and returns to the kitchen. She comes back with a bowl of olives, decorating several dishes with the olives.
VERENA: Be quiet for a moment—don't you hear something?
She listens. The Writer reads.

VERENA: The sound of rushing water. Turn off your recorder. Draga has a bladder problem—she goes to the bathroom thirty times a day.
The Writer reads on. Verena watches him. She goes behind the easy chair and places her hands on his chest.
VERENA: Now I need you to put down your book and look at me.
He puts down his book and turns around.
VERENA: Now I need you to write a poem—right now—you can do that well enough, but you have to use the word "joy" in your poem.
WRITER: Poem, Poem, Go hoem—you give me no joy because I stand to suffer when I try to rhyme your lines. Take the book.
She takes the book that he had put down. Title: Cultural Criticism in the Context of the Times. She sits down next to him.
WRITER: Read this part here aloud, please.
The Writer lays his head in Verena's lap. With cheeks puffed out he blows air between her legs. Verena reads.
VERENA: "Once again a product that shames our times. What brain is possessed by a human being that can create such nonsense and then allow it to be produced on stage? And what must it look like inside that brain and heart which regards such creations of his soul with such praise? To write like that is to trample good taste and healthy criticism underfoot— nothing but endless pages of disgusting repetition of the most vulgar expressions. Everything this writer touches turns empty and base."
WRITER: Read on, please read on.
VERENA: Philipp Moritz on the premiere of Schiller's *Intrigue and Love*—Berlin, Voss' Journal.
Verena jumps up and hurries into the kitchen. She returns with a bowl of mayonnaise.
VERENA: Is the tape recorder on? If you really want to understand who I am, you have to ask me—Who am I? Who am I?
WRITER: Into the mike, otherwise you lose the sound.
He holds up the microphone to her. She sits next to him. She holds the mayonnaise bowl in her lap.
VERENA: You know I am always asking myself why I exist,

what's my role here, what can I do? It's like I'm on a ship and I look for the stars to tell me where's north, where's south?
He bends his head down into the mayonnaise bowl. Verena pushes him aside and goes over to the buffet table.
VERENA: It's like I'm always searching for something. I like to read books about couples' relationships—psychological, maybe I'm a scientific person.
Silence. She takes a knife.
VERENA: What would you say if I took this knife and ruined these nice expensive hors d'oeuvres? What were we talking 'bout?
WRITER: You were in a boat and searching . . .
VERENA: Oh yes. You've known him for years and also know he's always having affairs. Do you think it's pleasant for me to find hotel bills for double rooms in his pocket after every medical convention he attends? He always tells me he feels hemmed in by me, but he's wrong if he thinks I'm holding him back. I'm the one who thinks the relationship is important but I'm not the one who holds him back. I have the feeling he always has to lean out of the boat to see what's going on and he doesn't even notice I'm sitting in front of him.
WRITER: And what about you? What do you want?
VERENA: Of course I try to use him for something. I'd like for him to be something—he won't do anything with me so I try to do something with him.
She laughs.
VERENA: Ultimately I'd like for him to continue to bring home as much money as possible so that I can live in peace. He's responsible for the money, I'm responsible for the home. And what about you? What do you want? What's going to come out in this play?
She places the knife at his throat and laughs.
VERENA: Who am I in your play?
Gustave Schneider comes out of the anteroom into the living room. He carries a doctor's "black bag" then puts it aside.
SCHNEIDER: *(laughing)* What! Are you going to murder our guest! Hello everyone. D'you wanna know what the problem was? The Philippine ambassador's son had a stomach-ache—that

was the cause of the whole excitement.
VERENA: He should make a poem out of it—he does that so well!
SCHNEIDER: OK, pal, let's go—Diagnosis: overeating. Result: The Philippine ambassador's son has a stomach-ache. In free verse.
Writer takes a drink from a whiskey bottle.
WRITER: In Marcos prisons
    Hunger climbs the walls
    Death cries
    In the early dawn
    Its message lost in the
    Cackling of the birds of paradise
    Torture and tourism is the Filipino
    Order of the day
    Evenings are
    Fiestas by the pool
    And curfew among the tin-roofed shacks
    We lie in darkness amid grime
    In sunlight on chaise lounges
    Gluttony and hunger
    Death
    And gluttony.
    The cries of the mourning parents are loud.
    For the ambassador's son
    Has a stomach-ache.
The two applaud. Schneider gives his wife a kiss.
SCHNEIDER: Make yourself pretty for tonight, OK, dear?
Verena climbs the stairs to a room upstairs.
SCHNEIDER: How's it going with your play about the rich and famous?
The Writer holds out the microphone. The elder Schneider enters the living room through the garden door. He is in a wheelchair and wears a robe. The Writer and Schneider fail to notice him.
SCHNEIDER: (*laughing into the microphone*) Give it here. Life is senseless. The world is senseless. The middle classes are senseless. The universe is senseless—and medicine is senseless.
He turns off the recorder and begins to tickle the Writer.

A Social Engagement   89

SCHNEIDER: There is an exception: An eighteen year old nurse's assistant named Hansi. You know I like to have these little detours where women are concerned.
The Elder Schneider rolls towards the two.
ELDER: There is no more decency in this country—no middle-class political party, only those who really think the security gate around this house will somehow keep them from turning into the mindless dwarfs they already are.
SCHNEIDER: Ah, good that you're here, Dad. I need to speak with you.
ELDER: *(to Writer)* What d'you think of the new Pope? If his holiness—this cure-all curate of modern television—had been a country priest in Ireland, maybe the wind would have frozen his loose tongue a little.
SCHNEIDER: Dad, he's busy.
ELDER: You're writing a play about society, eh? What do you know about society?
He begins to groan and grab his side.
ELDER: I make a distinction between doctors and physicians. Physicians are ethical; doctors are butchers. My son is a typical doctor, and says I have cancer . . . He always wants to talk to me about money. Here—touch this spot on me—You see, heaven dwells there already—this growing God—the garden of Eden grows here—a stinking swamp—and my soul will wallow in it just like a pig in his sty. What's the matter? What's so awful about it? What right do we have to demand that heaven should be pretty? How could we have deserved something like that? We who wear the mark of Cain on our foreheads—a race of fratricides. Man is civil war, family is civil war, the society is civil war! Our people are armed to the teeth and wound everything that gets in their way. Our people? Society, you say? I've got a lot to tell you about their brand of social consciousness! Where I went to school—not the academy, they called it a Jewish school—I got by by the skin of my teeth—long after they flunked Franz Schubert for math. Underclassman Schnitzler, Underclassman Hofmannsthal—my classmates Oppenheim and Edelmann—in our burning hearts we bore the ABCs of tomorrow's literary masterpieces—living citizenship—not asocial or anti-Semitic—my people with their Reformer's club for the preser-

vation of social issues—the Society to combat anti-Semitism—ever heard of it? Don't worry, I'll get to the present in a moment. No one has any patience nowadays . . . then there were the damn Christian Socialists—not really Christian, they just went to church all the time. They owned all the big estates, lame souls, all—and the Socialist clique in the Town Hall—even then they betrayed workers, they insulted farmers! And the Christian Democrats with their private militias; the socialists with their dreams of merging with Germany! They betrayed us . . . wore us down, beat us down, stepped on us and served us Herr Adolf on a silver platter. The burning hearts of my friends—the burning ovens. Wait a minute, I'll be in the present soon. Christian Oppenheim—Theresienstadt; Simon Edelmann—Auschwitz . . . From class to gas, from the library to the concentration camp. (*screams*) The final solution to the Jewish question was the greatest step toward the final solution of the mankind question—Heaven and Earth are dissolved; God's burned alive in the burning brush and afterwards—in view of the cold ovens—the world has lost all trace of a comforting shadow.

He holds his side and groans.

SCHNEIDER: Dad, are you taking your medicine?
ELDER: The present . . . This country was never rebuilt. It died under the weight of the new alphabet. Illiterate peoples founded incredible cultures yet they never created atrocities like the moderns. An alphabet: a language which takes a false step is destroyed. Trade union lingo, business lingo, school lingo, lingo lingo—it's barbarous. Language is the expression of the self's openness. A mighty fortress behind which the soul vegetates . . . the ruling Social Democrats—a church without a faith—a non-concert for a non-orchestra. Along with prominent academics you've got your young party functionary who always hangs around as well—a bunch of unmusical slobs—the party offers them a shelter from the storm—security from the dawn of faith, from the dawn of Utopia, security from God—God—who's always in front of me, yet is never reachable. The forty-year-olds of today—my God—they wear gold masks during the day and blubber helplessly at night . . . A sheltered generation of big-time criminals. They stand in the desert, in the jungle, in the cities, before

the great secrets of our own brains and presume to explain heaven and earth—and with what result? The sewage—their sewage stinks the same . . . technologized or Nazified . . . they're the friends of Goebbels, who wanted to look at Stalingrad like some big beautiful painting. Hitler didn't want to talk about it but today's architects . . . they are all like Goebbels—he, at least, studied philosophy—they just read about economics and medicine—am I still honorary head of the Academy? Drive them out, these future doctors, lawyers and politicians! Get them out of their studies—they run the risk of turning out like my son! In fifty thousand years the temples were built open to the skies so that the rain could fill them up—and it falls everywhere—open below, open on the left—left, where the heart beats . . . it won't beat much longer for me—now I'd like to take a moment to ask a question . . . when can we eat? I'm starved!

Blackout—Music

Scene Two

Thirty minutes later—the same room. The sun begins to set in the garden. Heiner Schneider, son of the Doctor, sits cross-legged on the couch beneath the stairs. He sits with his cassette recorder, listening to music through earphones. The Writer and Gustave Schneider sit in easy chairs in front of the window. In front of them—a reel-to-reel recorder with microphone.

SCHNEIDER: My first wife had an ovarian cyst. We thought at first it was a tubular pregnancy but the diagnosis came out endometriosis. That's a slow, progressive problem. The past interests you, really?
Writer nods.
SCHNEIDER: Anyway, sexuality is really something bad, something sinful—she held it for ransom—that was her sadistic side. She became a strange person—anthropologically speaking, a real health nut. And my, er, "need" for younger women was, even back then . . . I built up this need from the most delicate spot—my wife's insufficiency. Pretty brutal, eh?
Schneider turns off the recorder.
SCHNEIDER: Listen, just between us. Do you have a thing with my wife?
WRITER: What makes you say that?
SCHNEIDER: It would really bother me with you. Maybe not as much if I didn't know you. But you—since I know you my imagination goes crazy. D'you know what—I'll make a suggestion—between brothers, so to speak, you leave my wife alone and I won't touch your girlfriends, OK?
The Writer turns back on the recorder.
WRITER: OK.
SCHNEIDER: I really love her but the crazy part of it is that without her I'd have no need for other women. Is that on tape? What were we talking about?
WRITER: Love, work, politics . . .
SCHNEIDER: Politically speaking, you might say I'm caught between different power blocks. The Socialists, of course, don't want doctors to make profits, don't want them in private

practice or to have any privileges. Private initiative like I have doesn't seem to promote Socialist thinking. Socialized medicine has restricted money-making and now one is forced into private practice—uterus . . . gall-bladder . . . appendix —out they come!
Silence
SCHNEIDER: What's wrong? Where is your imagination?
WRITER: What? Oh yeah . . . Sure, I do find that kind of medicine pretty shitty.
SCHNEIDER: Me too. But that's reality. Does the same thing happen to you—I mean—that you can really imagine how your wife sleeps with other men? How they hold her, her breast, her vagina—how they do it—better than you, probably. Don't you ever have those fantasies?
Schneider tickles the Writer and laughs.
SCHNEIDER: As a man you're kind of interchangeable—accidental. Whenever I sleep with other women I'm involved but not really—it just means less. But that's off the record—OK? I believe we were talking about gall-bladders. Look—everyone accuses me of turning medicine into a business, but there are so many in every city who need services like mine and who can afford them. If they don't get them from me they can get them from somebody else. After all, medicine is a source of income like anything else. It's all the better service for the money you can put into it. We must, and I regard this as our chief task, see to it that the populace in general invests more and more in maintaining their level of good health. And what the public health offices spend—we would argue—in no way guarantees one proper health. Which is linked to a certain percentage of the Gross National Product and that ought to rise—in turn with everything else—when people's earning power also rises. It's just that I can't treat a patient as well when I know that he has so and so much money socked away and he hands me a voucher from the public health service. But on the other hand—when you've got a Turkish migrant worker's son sitting in front of you—he gets better care 'cause I've got connections with the outpatient clinic where they can be persuaded to do that stuff for free. The recorder makes me nervous, to tell you the truth.
The Writer turns off the recorder. Schneider leans back, closes

his eyes and lays his hand on the Writer's shoulder.
SCHNEIDER: I've always dreamed that I am an adventurer at heart
—a hero, a knight, a knight in shining armor.
Silence
SCHNEIDER: I am the knight who rescues the beautiful damsel in distress, something like that.
Silence. The Writer turns back on the tape recorder.
SCHNEIDER: I buy comic books—all that I can get new, old . . . and when I read them then I have this funny association with my childhood—then I can sleep peacefully and somehow I'm happy. If I can get a hold of a new copy of Uncle Scrooge and Donald—my whole evening is complete.
Schneider notices that the recorder continues to turn; he turns it off.
SCHNEIDER: Actually, I'm all alone in this forlorn reality. What does she want from me? Do you understand her? My son attends the most expensive private school there is, she lives in this elegant villa—what more could she want? By the way, I've got an interesting job for my spare time—I give checkups to managers of multinational corporations. When one gets sick—in any way—he tumbles down the ladder of success—no mercy.
The Writer turns the recorder on again.
SCHNEIDER: The business with the clinic for the terminally ill goes pretty well. We're buying the old restaurant in the Kahlenberg Heights and are going to renovate completely—a kind of luxury hotel for rich dying old ladies. (*He laughs*) I need money from the old man for the investment. Have you noticed how he's getting crazier all the time? And then sometimes he's fine and fakes it whenever I want money from him. D'you know what my wife wants me to do? What bothers her about me? "The emotional element." Emotion. Emotion. Emotion. I can't hear it anymore—the word drives me nuts. Doesn't anyone here realize I have feelings too, that I'm sensitive too?!
He turns off the recorder, then rewinds it a bit.
TAPE: . . . Emotion. Emotion. Emotion. Doesn't anyone here realize I have feelings too, that I'm sensitive too?!
He laughs and lets the tape continue.
SCHNEIDER: Shit. Look—the Physician. You have to establish so

many medical centers for the poor, we do have them, you know, for the underprivileged and the working poor, centers where only they are allowed to go. They have them in America too—unemployed, the helpless and limited income pensioners . . . . Well, I'm talking like an anti-Socialist again—they don't want anything like an underclass—although it's only logical. What they call socialism these days is really nothing like socialism—you'll agree to that won't you?

WRITER: Sure.

SCHNEIDER: Sure. This kind of discussion with you really helps me. We don't do this often enough, you and I. What I'd really like to do is live on an island, swim in the sea—but after two or three weeks I'd probably miss the challenges.

Silence

SCHNEIDER: My favorite is the healthy patient whose health I reaffirm. That guy is thankful for the good news and pays gladly to get it. Really sick, helpless patients are no fun to treat for everyone—what's the challenge in something like that? That's why cancer patients wander all around Robin Hood's barn—every doctor turns them down—no challenge in them.

Silence. Schneider playfully boxes with the Writer.

SCHNEIDER: Tell me, am I a good guy or a bad guy in your play?

The Elder Schneider in the wheelchair enters from the garden and moves to the buffet table. He takes a spoon and begins to eat right from the serving dishes. Schneider jumps up and knocks the spoon from the Elder Schneider's hand.

SCHNEIDER: (*screaming at him*) Are you crazy?! You know good and well you have to keep to your diet!!

ELDER: Doesn't anyone here listen to the radio? 30 people killed on the highway in one weekend—mostly young kids from the country . . .

The Elder Schneider clutches his side.

ELDER: From the abandoned villages the souls of young boys cry out in agony, the souls of young boys who have wrapped their cars around trees—doesn't that bother anyone? Necessity sent them on their way, drink ended their trip . . . out of the forests the dark screams of the discotheques draw new victims to the depths. There is no longer a roadside unwashed *in young blood—it's all covered in mud, soaked with gore. Schneider pushes the Elder Schneider back out into the garden. He returns, goes to the stairway and observes his son, who still sits cross-legged listening to his cassettes on the couch. Schneider returns to the Writer and sits behind him.*

SCHNEIDER: Is it running? Do you remember the check-up I had done on myself when I had the kidney problems? The enemas! There is nothing as humiliating as an enema and then running to the toilet—Jesus—the toilets in the community hospitals are always full—that's where all the prostate cases are—it was torture for me. Horrible. The doctor as Patient—never again.
Silence

SCHNEIDER: Have you also noticed that my son is getting so cynical? I've been paying his therapy bills now for over a year but I don't think it's getting any better.
Silence

SCHNEIDER: I've tried everything. I try to develop logical reasons, I live responsibly—and hope privately that the two types of examples will have some kind of positive effect on him. Maybe I ought to just give him orders.
Silence

SCHNEIDER: Presumably the first three years which he spent so much of with his mother, my first wife—before she turned so strange—those three years were decisive for him. But I had to work—my career was important for him, too—that he ends up somewhere where there are some advantages.
Silence

SCHNEIDER: The setback with my son—it really is something painful—you might say it's the worst setback I've ever had. A doctor is like a priest . . . or a writer. I think doctors shouldn't marry. (*He laughs.*) How do your girlfriends spend their time?

WRITER: Wait a minute.
He checks the tape.

WRITER: It's OK.
Silence

SCHNEIDER: In general I would say that I'm satisfied if I can work and earn money. The only problem is that I'm not up to date culturally. I've been buying up books for months on

modern literature—but I don't get the chance to read them. At the moment I'm tiding the wave of mysticism—I buy up everything on religions and rituals from the Far East.
Silence. Schneider turns the recorder off.
SCHNEIDER: You will probably think I'm crazy when I tell you I want to draw up a contract with my wife. In writing I want her to guarantee that she won't leave me. After all she's still dependent on me financially—she can't divorce me, she doesn't have a profession—what would she do? Don't you think so?
The Writer turns the recorder on again. Silence.
SCHNEIDER: Have I ever told you about my experiences as a young intern? I was very infantile then. I felt I had to help absolutely every and anyone who had a problem. I was called to OB/GYN—a woman had just delivered her third child—then her heart stopped. I tried heart massage and was still at it when they said I could stop—she was dead. Her husband was in the waiting room—eager for the happy news. I went out with the head doctor—he told him. I'll never forget the husband's face . . . really . . . . I'll never forget it. The reality is that ultimately you're helpless.
He laughs.
SCHNEIDER: The best thing to do is to crawl back into childhood. I mean, I can remember days, Sundays, when I set up my castles and knights in the garden, laid my head in the grass and all my problems simply fell away. Well, the point of all this I haven't even mentioned. My wife wants to divorce—for good. This party is s'posed to be a kind of "going away" party—neat idea, eh?
Verena appears on the stairs. She is "quite well turned out." Schneider looks up at her and laughs.
SCHNEIDER: *(laughing)* Wonderful, my dear.

Blackout—music.

Scene Three

Fifteen minutes later—the same room. The Garden has been strung with electric lanterns. Heiner Schneider, the Doctor's son, sits cross-legged in an easy chair under the stairs. He wears earphones while listening to his cassette recorder. The Writer and Verena Schneider also sit in easy chairs. Verena sips now and then at her drink.

VERENA: Did you see this film? There's this big power—at the head of it all a machine, a lord, a god, masked, black, shining, distant and cold—a robot. Whoever doesn't work is killed immediately and he falls right over dead. And then there are the rebels who fight against the system—they have a woman as their leader, a princess who holds power over the people in a decent, honest manner. I am trying to understand the way men live, so to speak, but I don't understand them. I live in constant dissonance with them.
Silence. Verena stands up, goes over to the stereo set, puts on a cassette of dance music. She moves to the rhythm of the music.
VERENA: For me it would be important, I don't know, that we sit down together, sing together, go to the theater together or don't go to the theater together, just live.
Silence. Verena places herself behind the Writer.
VERENA: Do you know what he thinks life with me is? Sex. Not that I am against it—but with every caress I already know how things will end up. It's all so goal-oriented. Men always seem to have this idea with women that they have to show them how great they are, that they've got a hard-on, so to speak.
The Writer takes the microphone and holds it high—towards her face. She bends down over him and turns off the recorder. She rewinds the tape.
SCHNEIDER'S VOICE: . . . The reality is that, ultimately, you're helpless.
Silence.
SCHNEIDER'S VOICE: The best thing to do would be to crawl back into childhood. I mean, I can remember days, Sundays, when

I set up my castles and knights in the garden, laid my head in the grass and all my problems simply fell away. Well, the point of all this I haven't even mentioned. My wife wants a divorce—for good. This party is s'posed to be a kind of "going away" party—neat idea, eh?
Silence.
SCHNEIDER'S VOICE: Wonderful my dear.
Verena turns the recorder off. She sits in the easy chair and stares off into space. She drinks her cocktail in one gulp. The Writer turns the tape recorder back on, pressing fast forward.
VERENA: Are you just interested in your play? What about me? I mean, as a person? Sometimes you remind me of my husband—he always expresses his interest for me but I don't feel anything emotionally.
The Writer turns the recorder off and lays his head in Verena's lap. He blows air between her legs. Gustave Schneider appears at the top of the stairs—he's wearing a dark suit with a white sweater. He regards the two briefly.
SCHNEIDER: Verena, dear, be a sweetheart and put on some decent music—something classical—but muted, please.
Verena gets up quickly and puts in a cassette of classical music. Schneider comes down the stairs into the room.
SCHNEIDER: (*To Writer*) And you, my friend, could I ask you to put away your genealogical research for awhile, eh? And should you feel the urge—after a few drinks—to insert one of your melodramatic commentaries I would also ask you to refrain—as there are several among those invited for tonight with whom I have to discuss certain business matters—OK? Do me that favor, please?
Verena curtsies.
VERENA: Is that all right?
Draga, the Yugoslav maid, brings drinks into the garden. She stops at the doorway that leads into the garden and observes the scene.
Schneider goes over to Verena and boxes her ears.
Verena laughs.
SCHNEIDER: (*to Draga*) What are you standing around here like an idiot for—Get things set up in the garden.
Draga carries the drinks into the garden. Schneider goes to the stairs and regards his son—who still sits cross-legged on

the couch listening to his tape player.
SCHNEIDER: Could I ask my dear son if he would please go get changed. Can you hear me? Turn that damn thing off!
The Elder Schneider in wheelchair comes out of the garden and goes over to the record player. He turns up the volume of the classical music.
ELDER: Hitler has risen again in the quiet corridors of art—his deputies drive away the proud, the creative into the cellar; the sirens of reproduction howl across the city—Reproduced! Reproduced! Everything in this country is reproduced! They feed at the trough of the same old line, of the same old plays—their swelled sense of art bloats dangerously. Souls are slaughtered but they stare still at pigs' eyes and sheep's ears along the stage. Philharmonic fascism drums and announces itself through the houses of art!
The Elder Schneider rolls over to the buffet table and begins to eat from a serving dish. Schneider runs to the stereo, turns off the music, pushes the Elder Schneider away from the buffet table and back into the garden. Schneider returns to the living room, goes over to his son, grabbing him under the arms and pulling him off the couch. Heiner lets himself be pulled about by his father like an empty sack. Schneider pulls his son up to the first steps of the stairs. The doorbell rings. Schneider lets go of his son and goes quickly to the anteroom. The front door opens. Schneider returns to the living room.
SCHNEIDER: (*To the Writer*) Did you invite this gentleman?
Behind Schneider there appears an actor. The actor wears a Christ beard and is dressed rather ostentatiously.
ACTOR: (*he speaks with a slight Italian accent*) Excuse me, I am very shy. Only in my craft do I open up, excuse me.
The Actor holds out a nylon sack with noodles to Schneider.
SCHNEIDER: What's this?
ACTOR: Taglieatelle Verde. A gift, excuse me—my mother sends me some every month from Calabrini—for you.
Schneider takes the noodles. The Actor opens his jacket and pulls out a gigantic torch. He takes a cigarette lighter from his pocket and lights the torch. The torch burns. He gives it to Verena.
ACTOR: Excuse me, for you. An expression of my burning devotion.

Verena takes the torch and holds it out for her. The Actor goes to the Writer and shakes his hand with both of his hands.
ACTOR: With art there are no gifts—just the truth. Excuse me.
VERENA: (*to Draga, the Yugoslav maid*) Draga, put this in the champagne cooler, please.
Draga takes the burning torch and goes, shaking her head into the garden.
SCHNEIDER: (*to the Actor*) If you would like something to drink—please, help yourself in the garden.
The Actor moves to the door, accompanied by smiles and much head-nodding.)
SCHNEIDER: (*to the Writer*) Tell me, who is this nut?
The Actor turns around in the doorway.
ACTOR: Evening is the transfiguration of day, excuse me.
The Actor exits into the garden.
WRITER: An original. He's heard that I'm writing a new play and wants a part in it at all costs. Besides, I've convinced him that he'll meet important people here tonight. Theater managers and people like that . . .
SCHNEIDER: I would have preferred a more famous actor.
WRITER: You've gotta give the new guys a chance, too.
The Elder Schneider returns from the garden to the living room, still in his wheelchair. He holds the torch in his hand and moves in the direction of the buffet tables.
ELDER: (*holding high the burning torch*) The provocation of thought heats up and burns away and disappears as lost smoke over the roofs and fields of our country. Truth has been divvied up so that it's biting smoke can dissolve into nothingness with ease . . . . The talented liar Franz Strauss, who calls himself Franz Josef since one nobleman tugged him from one slaughterhouse to another, . . . the missile is always dangerous. Murders always stand in the middle and the middle is the lamb of the false god.
Schneider lunges at the Elder, turns the wheelchair violently about and pushes the Elder quickly back into the garden. The Writer and Verena look at each other.
VERENA: Sometimes you seem like a person who never helps out. You always just watch and listen.
The Writer lays his head on Verena's lap—she pushes him away.

VERENA: Stop it.
The Writer regards Verena, stands up, goes over to the buffet table, kneels before the table and sticks his head in the mayonnaise bowl. The doorbell. Verena goes quickly to answer the door. Schneider comes back from the garden into the living room. He holds the smoking torch.

SCHNEIDER: I've locked him away. I've just locked him away for awhile.
Verena appears in the living room, behind her the Filipino guests—two men and two women.

VERENA: (*to Schneider*) Did you invite these people?

SCHNEIDER: (*approaches Filipinos, holding the smoldering torch—smiling, in a friendly tone of voice*) How are you? How is your lovely child?

FILIPINO: (*with a glance at the smoking torch and the mayonnaise smeared face of the kneeling Writer*) Are we too early?

Blackout—Music.

Scene Four

Forty-five minutes later—the same room. Evening. The garden has been strung with electric lanterns. Most of the guests have moved to the garden. The four Filipino guests stand around awkwardly in the living room, glass in hand and silent. Heiner, the Doctor's son, wearing a dark suit, also stands awkwardly, glass in hand. The buffet table has been picked at to a certain extent. Muted, classical music.

The Writer and Theater Producer—come from the garden into the living room and go to the buffet table.

PRODUCER: If the people would just play their roles decently—but they don't do that. Girls don't play Diabelli anymore. Dusty old vases stand on deserted pianos—a sure sign that no one uses the piano. They can't make conversation anymore—they can't even bake anymore, not to mention knowing how to sit or conduct oneself in a way to delight us—charm, attractiveness, erotic—nothing.

They move to the buffet table; the Producer serves himself. The Entrepreneur's wife comes from the garden to the buffet table.

PRODUCER: All this Marxism, class warfare and shit—those are passé, quite frankly I think we need to divide up people in quite different categories, say, into smart and dumb groups—or into educated and ignorant. If you're writing about the middle class then I'd advise you to forget it. Write about the unions. They have the real power nowadays.

WIFE: *(follows them)* We also have the interesting problem that the high rate of taxation for the wealthy really does very little, fiscally speaking.

PRODUCER: *(does not react to the woman; instead he continues to speak with the Writer)* My grandparents always used to set something aside for the poor. The thing that bothers me about socialism is that it doesn't allow for poverty. Poverty—the worthiest human activity—seeking and begging, something every kid can do—that's against the law in socialism.

WIFE: In every society that I've seen so far there have been some people who are better off than others. That's just the way things are, I guess—human nature. I've seen it in Mao's China, in Africa, there where the size of the group is only 50 originally—more join in, the numbers rise, sure enough, whether it's families or just individuals, there are those who are different, who have other opportunities than most. People who are lucky, who are talented beyond the average level always move away from the crowd. It would be unthinkable to distribute the wealth equally to all sections of society.

PRODUCER: (*to the Writer*) As far as the Socialists go—they've already begun their dance around the golden calf. You've got these Philistines, these accountants and such—people who are really low-life—spiritually and materially—and they're the ones climbing into Mercedes and running the world. They sit in the capitals in palaces like kings—they've got the political power, but no intellectual power to go with it. Culture and esprit and style—those are things passed down through generations. In my opinion, a kid gets that in the sperm that creates him, or the genes or his mother's milk.

The writer and producer move to the door which leads to the garden.

WIFE: (*follows them*) We do have the problem that the high rate of taxation for the wealthy really does very little, fiscally speaking.

The writer, the producer, and the entrepreneur's wife go into the garden.

Gustave Schneider comes from the garden into the living room.

SCHNEIDER: (*to one of the Filipinos*) Are you fine?

FILIPINO: Thank you, very fine.

Schneider goes over to his son.

SCHNEIDER: Don't just stand around—go make conversation with the folks. You can speak English, can't you?

He takes his son by the hand and leads him to a Filipino.

SCHNEIDER: May I introduce you to my son?

FILIPINO: (*To Heiner*) How do you do?

SCHNEIDER: (*To Filipino*) Excuse me.

Schneider returns to the garden. The Filipino and Heiner stand across from each other in silence. Draga, the Yugoslav housekeeper, enters with a large serving tray full of empty

glasses. She comes from the garden and is heading for the kitchen. Heiner goes over to her, intending to help; but Draga moves past him into the kitchen.
Schneider comes with the Member of Parliament out of the garden into the living room. They move to the buffet table. Schneider helps him fill his plate.

SCHNEIDER: Do you like olives? I guess you have to—it's kind of a political necessity, right? You know, this clinic we're planning will be affordable for almost everyone; so there won't be a question whether people with, let's say, low incomes will be able to be treated there. In fact, the possibility exists that they can spend their twilight years with access to first-class medical facilities—we would just have to clear things with the appropriate public health offices. The problem seems to be the manner by which some state funds can be rededicated in the budget. Roast beef?

Silence. Schneider looks at the politicians.

SCHNEIDER: As a Socialist Member of Parliament, your influence in budgetary matters naturally is substantial.

Schneider laughs. The politician laughs likewise.

MP: Doctor, that reminds me of a joke—at the Royal Court in Poland one day, a Jewish trader says to an Austrian Army officer—"My God, Mr. Austrian Officer, that's awful." "Indeed? What is so awful?" the Austrian says. "Well," the Jew replies, "Look—with the Russian officers one knows good and well they're corrupt: with the Prussian officers, one is sure they are not corrupt; but with the Austrians, one never knows—are they corrupt, are they not corrupt . . . . Since then it seems we've become more like the Russians than the Prussians."

The two retire back into the garden.
The Filipinos and Heiner stand about the living room in silence.
The Writer enters the living room with the producer, behind them—the Entrepreneur's wife. She appears rather matronly—dressed in an Austrian folk costume.

PRODUCER: *(to Writer)* I'd do it gladly if I only knew what it was.

WRITER: Generally speaking—about you.

They sit on the couch under the stairs. The writer sets up the

recorder. The Producer's wife sits down next to the Producer.
WRITER: Please, go ahead.
Silence
PRODUCER: For example, this will give you a good idea of me. I've always found it terrible that Hilary wouldn't let Sherpa Tensing stay in the tent with him at their last encampment before going to the top of Everest. Tensing had to sleep outside in a sleeping bag.
PRODUCER'S WIFE: It's very difficult for my husband.
She takes his hand, he pulls it away from her.
PRODUCER: Personal stuff, too?
The Writer nods.
PRODUCER: Personally, I come from a family in which the differences of being, to use Schopenhauer's phrase, the differences of being of my parents was a problem for the children—that is, the obvious tensions between a rather Bohemian mother and a strict Catholic father—you've heard of the brewing company, I'm sure . . . .
Silence
PRODUCER: When my father died they gave him one of the most extravagant burials in the town's history. Everybody who was anybody in business was there, the minister of commerce, too. And the next day I was left alone. It was clear to me that the world had little interest in me—and I wasn't interested in brewing beer, either.
Silence. The Producer's wife takes his hand; he pulls it away.
PRODUCER: I was always a rebel in this society—always a fighter and that's why it's somewhat unusual that I ended up here as a producer. I've spent my whole life wishing—that's my present function—trying to create opportunities for other people to display their human and creative talents. You see, there was never anyone like that for me.
WIFE: It was very difficult for my husband.
She takes his hand, he pulls it away. This occurs totally automatically.
PRODUCER: From my very nature I've always been—and excuse me if I use an often misused word—I've been a leader. It seems my natural role. At Catholic boarding school I jumped up on the table and screamed at the top of my lungs, "I am the devil, I am the devil!" And everyone ran out the door—

those "good" little boys in their sailor suits.
Silence.
PRODUCER: As a family we were very strongly anti-fascist—I've got the documents to prove it.
Silence.
PRODUCER: You know what they say about God or Nature or whatever is making everyone equal—that's really not true, they're not.
Verena enters the room. She observes the Writer as he interviews the Producer, goes to the stereo set, stops the cassette of classical music, and goes to put a new one in. Rock music is heard. Verena turns the stereo very loud.
PRODUCER: The complete mixing-up of everything—this computerized version of the individual . . .
The woman takes his hand, he pulls it away. The rock music is so loud that he is forced almost to shout in order to make himself heard.
PRODUCER: It's really not a long leap to concentration camps again. You just need to add a little bit to socialism and you get National Socialism. Things have simply become unbelievable —everyone the same, like Rudolf von Habsburg says, doesn't make them equal just more lowly.
Verena bows before the writer. She holds a glass.
PRODUCER: *(almost shouting)* Inequality! Yes, inequality! There is such a thing. From birth I've been humpbacked.
WIFE: It has been very difficult for my husband.
VERENA: *(to Writer)* Excuse me.
Schneider enters the room, quickly moves to the stereo set and stops the music. He takes Verena around the waist, removes the glass from her hand, and pulls her out into the garden. From behind, this action appears to be an embrace, rather than a forceful act.
The Entrepreneur enters from the garden. He appears to be a friendly type. He wears glasses and is always smiling. He stops in front of Schneider and his wife.
ENTREPRENEUR: *(interpreting Schneider's grip on his wife as an embrace)* And how long have you two been married? To each other? Love, love, to be able to love and believe that it is a blessing that you cannot buy. I have to admit—I have never been fresh or new or ever really in love. I mean, for me love

is action and reaction, impression and agitation. After all is said and done, we humans really are just a kind of metabolism-machine with entrances and exits. By the way, Doctor, if you would like that I take part in your clinic project I would advise you to push ahead with the thing. I can't commit the capital for a drawn-out length of time.

Schneider pulls Verena into the garden. The Entrepreneur goes over to Heiner. He speaks in an animated manner without waiting for the boy's reaction to his words.

ENTREPRENEUR: What's the problem with your generation? I just can't understand the ideas of today's young people—especially since I know for a fact that everyone has an equal chance in this country. We're given the opportunity to pull forward or go back in anything we want. Kids today rebel for biological reasons—it's kind of a stage of development they go through. One will speak his mind quietly, the other loudly, but I don't think there's really a problem. You can only really take them seriously from a political standpoint when they've achieved positions of responsibility. That's what we need, really, we'll change soon enough after that. You could even allow a few demonstrations—for nuts and crazies—it really wouldn't bother anyone as far as I'm concerned.

He looks around, moves from Heiner to one of the Filipinos.

ENTREPRENEUR: (*to Filipino*) It really bugs me when I see these people in developing countries lying about in the sun with their hands out and no desire to work. Life in industrial society is no bowl of cherries—we pay a high price for it—and these folks lie around with their wonderful weather. I like to go there for vacation. They don't have our prosperity but it doesn't seem to bother them. So I don't think it's right to feel guilty about the Third World. Enjoy what you've earned —you've paid a high price for it—for prosperity, I mean, even if it sounds a bit too insensitive. It's kind of schizophrenic when we run around feeling guilty, knowing all the while that there's nothing we can do unless we lower our own status.

The Filipino does not react.

ENTREPRENEUR: Our humanistic attitude in questions like this seems a bit too highfalutin'. Should I really worry if there is nothing I can do? It's too much to expect, really. Millions of

people are dying and here some guy spends his money so that one black or yellow kid can eat—that's pretty . . . Don't you think?
FILIPINO: How do you do?
Entrepreneur goes to the Writer who sits with the Producer and his Wife in front of the recorder.
ENTREPRENEUR: (*points to the recorder*) Can anyone join in on this parlor game? What are you talking about? I hope not about culture—if so I'll have to pass on that one. I've nothing to say there—I can't even find time to use my season tickets. You know these people, these artists who have something to say, I really admire them. Although you've got to admit that most of them idealize these things too much and are too unrealistic and caught up with their projects. But still you get the impression—Look, at least he believes in something—but on the other hand you could say that these guys are not all there—that they don't see reality . . . but maybe luck's on their side. Still, I think that as long as you've got no choice in the matter, you should just keep your mouth shut.
In the garden the actor has begun singing "Ave Maria." The Entrepreneur's wife comes out of the garden and locks her arm around that of her husband.
WIFE: (*smiling, to the Writer and Producer*) My husband is the CEO of the firm where we made our money, I am CEO of the firm which extends our cultural horizons.
She leads her husband into the garden. The sound of "Ave Maria" becomes louder and louder.
PRODUCER: (*to his Wife*) Go on to the garden, I'll be there in a second. Go on.
His Wife looks at him, stands up and goes into the garden.
PRODUCER: (*to Writer*) I could tell you of a certain Oedipal affair, when my father . . . You see, I worshiped this girl—a factory girl in the Christmas beer division. I even wrote a song to her . . . harmless . . . quite innocent . . . and my father fired her. I've experienced much and much much more!
WRITER: Just a moment—the tape.
The Writer rewinds the tape.
VOICE OF THE ENTREPRENEUR: " . . . But still, maybe luck's on their side . . . ."

The Writer winds the tape forward.
WRITER: Now.
PRODUCER: How can we artists—and I include myself here—explain our suffering to others? "You have diamonds and pearls, you have all that humans desire, you have the most beautiful eyes to go with them, darling, who could ask for anything more . . . . To your lovely eyes I have composed eternal songs . . . ." And so forth. That's a poem I wrote when I was fifteen. Can you imagine? Ever since I was born, ever since I had this humpback, I've had to say what a pig God has been to me. I never masturbated, never lied once, not even skipped school—and still I get punished—but I knew there was a greater righteousness than that on earth and I developed the idea that God did love me after all. I'm not looking at this masochistically—making a virtue of my handicap—believe me it's no virtue, it's a pain when you are left out at dance class. It's a great pain when even in the worst heat you can't take your coat off. My whole life has been a struggle—you have to help yourself so that God will help you. That's what separated me from the Socialists. As a Catholic I know that the world is unjust. The Socialists think that you can solve all the problems and erect some kind of Heaven on earth. You can't.
Verena comes out of the garden and into the living room. She is tipsy. "Ave Maria" is still being heard in the garden. Verena goes to the Writer and then the Producer. She looks at the writer. He switches the recorder off. Silence. The Producer looks at the Writer then at Verena.
VERENA: (*to Writer*) Please let's get out of here—I can't stand it anymore.
Verena embraces the Writer and holds him tightly. The Writer caresses her head.
VERENA: Please.
The Producer watches both of them.
PRODUCER: Anyone who has ever really been in love knows that love hurts.
Verena presses her head on the Writer's shoulder. The Writer caresses her. Silence.
PRODUCER: Sin is something important and something majestic. Nowadays mankind dispenses with the devil and sin and any

kind of polarity—everything done away with, without tension—a piece of misery, a piece of easily explainable flesh and blood . . . .
The Writer turns on the recorder behind Verena's back. The Producer carefully begins to caress Verena's back.
PRODUCER: I believe in the power of sin. Only those who fight with angels and gods—with their spirits—only those yearn—only those live, for life is guilt.
The Producer moves his hand down Verena's buttocks and over her hips.
PRODUCER: The great lover—the magician—the lover—he's an endangered species, a dinosaur.
The Producer draws closer to Verena and the Writer.
PRODUCER: Everything has become unbelievable—shells of words, empty metaphors—even a word like "intercourse" . . . that's so obscene and lascivious. How much more poetic is the word "fuck."
Gustave Schneider brings the Elder Schneider in a wheelchair back into the living room.
ELDER: Hunger!
The Producer jumps up and moves into the garden. The Writer pushes Verena aside. Verena takes his glass and drinks it up.
SCHNEIDER: (*to Elder*) Excuse me, Dad, that I locked you in your room. I was just really nervous and, well, you weren't exactly acting very gentlemanly before.
ELDER: Hunger!
Schneider leads the Elder Schneider to the buffet table and helps him serve himself.
SCHNEIDER: What'll it be, Dad? Listen, I really have to have a serious talk with you. The financing of the clinic is all set except for my share—
ELDER: More, more—some chicken, too.
SCHNEIDER: And I feel certain we'll get the public land, completely certain. Dad—the problem is that I need for you to sell the lakefront property so that I can pull my share.
ELDER: Mayonnaise.
SCHNEIDER: My inheritance from mother is also there. So the request does have its justification. Besides what do you want to do with the land anyway?
ELDER: Good fat pork, pork.

SCHNEIDER: Listen, Dad, you know that I can have you declared incompetent, don't you?

ELDER: Wonderful—tastes just wonderful.

The Actor returns to the living room, behind him come the other guests as well.

ACTOR: (*loudly, with pathos*) I shall play whatever you wish! Each second of my life is filled with tears and joys. Excuse me, I've had one success after the other, one glowing review after the other. What would you like? Goethe? Schiller? Shakespeare? I played in Italy and when there were hecklers in the audience I threw popcorn at them. I've thrown out journalists personally from several theaters. My mother phoned me from Calabrini—Mama—I see you just like thirty years ago. Of course, Mama—sure I still drink milk, don't worry, mama aren't you happy about my career, mama? Alas I've studied now Philosophy, Jurisprudence and sadly, too, theology through and through—with heart and soul—and here I stand a total fool—and know as much as if I never went to school—I'm called Master, even Doctor, too . . . .

Blackout—music.

Scene Five

Ten minutes later, all the guests are in the living room: The Member of Parliament, the Producer and his Wife, the Entrepreneur and his Wife, the four Filipinos as well as the family—Gustave Schneider, Verena and Heiner. The Elder Schneider is not present. In the background Draga carries in glasses and plates from the kitchen. The actor gives forth and jumps about on easy chairs and dining chairs.

ACTOR: (*Excerpt from Faust*)
  But would that I, on mountains grand,
  Amid thy blessed light could stand,
  With spirits through mountain-caverns hover,
  Float in thy twilight the meadows over,
  And, freed from the fumes of lore that swathe me,
  To health in thy dewy fountains bathe me!
  Ah, me! this dungeon still I see,
  This drear, accursed masonry,
  Where even the welcome daylight strains
  But duskly through the painted pains.
  Hemmed in by many a toppling heap
  Of books worm-eaten, gray with dust,
  Which to the vaulted ceiling creep,
  Against the smoky papers thrust,—
  With glasses, boxes, round me stacked,
  And instruments together hurled,
  Ancestral lumber, stuffed and packed—
  Such is my world: and what a world!
  And do I ask, wherefore my heart
  Falters, oppressed with unknown needs?
  Why some inexplicable smart
  All movement of my life impedes?
  The guests become inattentive, noisy.
WRITER: Why don't you act out your own life?
ACTOR: Excuse me, I hate this acting stuff, you know, all this pretending—it's all counterfeit anyway. I like to see myself as unchangeable even when I act.
WRITER: OK, go.

ACTOR: (*Stands on his chair, is completely unsure of himself*) Well, let's see, I was born in Calabrini in a small place they call Langobardi, a province of Cosenza. And I was always the greatest love of my mother's life—always.
PRODUCER: Bravo—but with more pathos.
ACTOR: (*beginning to act*) My father was very jealous since my mother was a very very good-looking woman. She couldn't even look out the window before father would pull her back —you know how it is.
PRODUCER: Keep going, keep going—stronger.
Several guests applaud and laugh.
ACTOR: So, in our living room there was a picture of a Mexican Christ—my mother sat in a chair the whole day and always looked at that picture—she had what you might call a relationship with that picture—in her imagination she wanted all her children to look like Christ. That's what I was—I became Christ for her.
Laughter and applause.
The Actor gestures that all should be quiet.
ACTOR: In 1946, if I remember correctly, the Germans came to Langobardi—five minutes before twelve. Two men came, pushed my mother onto the bed—I heard horrible sounds, horrible sounds.
ENTREPRENEUR: (*laughing*) Terrible!
ACTOR: You have to understand that my father was in America at that time and we went to America on the "Vulcania" —that's the name of the ship we were on. When we landed in America I said to my mother "What does father look like?" "Your father is a very handsome man," she said and I looked about and saw a man with chocolate bars waving to us. A very handsome man—even in Calabrini they used to say that he was the spitting image of Valentino—Rudolph Valentino, my father.
PRODUCER: I see, and his son's name was Jesus Christ.
Producer laughs.
ACTOR: By 1949 we were back in Italy and I went to the Salesians—a church school. I'd have to wake up at five o'clock and go to church with the others. They made me into a singer—I used to have a great singing voice.
He begins to sing "Ave Maria" again.

A Social Engagement 115

PRODUCER: Act, don't sing.
ACTOR: Excuse me, who hurts me, loses me, I'll go away and leave you alone.
Laughter.
ACTOR: I am a clown who sells paper flowers in the dark corner of the train station late at night.
Laughter and applause.
ACTOR: Once I stole communion bread and hid it in my shirt—I had a strong identification with Christ back then. They kicked me out, I was masturbating with the other boys. In 1956 my father took us back to America and he took us to the Bronx —that's the worst place on earth—it's murder.
Several guests move to the buffet table. Draga returns with a tray of filled glasses.
ACTOR: I went to bed and time passed. Then my mother pulled off the covers and started hitting me with a stick, and then she hit herself and cursed and I remember one of her breasts hanging out—all naked. I went to Theodore Roosevelt High School and had my first confrontation with blacks—they were called "colored" then. I saw a girl on the stairs, whose breast had been half cut away by a black guy—in cold blood.
Gustave Schneider goes to the stereo set, puts in a cassette— classical music is heard.
ACTOR: I was never really brought up, never really loved—just bigotry, that's all I saw. At the beginning of 1958 I went to the Young Men's Club and came home too late. I rang the bell and my mother told me through a crack in the door that my father had forbidden her to open the door for me. They put cotton in the bell. I sat on the steps until I got really tired. Then this young guy came along—Murphy was his name, he was a mailman—and he told me not to worry, he'd take me home. So I went home with this Murphy guy and smoked a cigarette holding it with two hands. Like this. I didn't know that it was marijuana, I was still innocent. That's the first time that I was arrested.
The guests divide up into groups and pairs.
ENTREPRENEUR: (*to MP*) To come back to what we were talking about—it's ridiculous to attack ideologies with clear argument—otherwise communism wouldn't exist. It's been proven that the free market is the only parameter—in other words

the market price—demand and supply coordinate well.
ACTOR: (*struggling against the emerging indifference*) They tied me to a chair and hit me—they hit me a lot over and over. Then my father paid my bail—see what happens when you come home late, he said.
The Actor kneels and hits himself. The Entrepreneur's Wife watches.
ENTREPRENEUR: (*to MP*) Communism shouldn't exist at all. They presuppose an ideal kind of man—homo idealis instead of homo oeconomicus or whatever, I'm not very good at Latin.
MP: It's the rather sad realization that the new man, whom the Socialists dreamed of at the century's beginning, simply is not going to come. It is not in our nature to be like that.
ACTOR: I had a crisis and wanted to live alone. I got a room for sixteen dollars a week and shared it with someone else.
The Entrepreneur's wife moves to help the Actor, he gestures her away.
MP: A society cannot function—you're exactly right—if it does not allow individual initiative for the areas of politics and economics. It just won't work unless you calculate desire for profit into the equation—without a doubt that's what the liberals in our movement just won't accept.
ACTOR: (*screams*) We had a party—like this one—a lot of people came, and suddenly there was this girl, she had taken a gun from her boyfriend's pocket and was playing around with it—the gun was loaded and she shot my roommate dead. They arrested me as an accessory to the crime—because I had been arrested before. This time I landed in an insane asylum—America has all these weird laws.
Verena sips from half-filled glasses, which stand around on tables. She goes to the stereo set, puts in a cassette of rock music, and turns the volume up slowly.
ACTOR: A great big white room. The first one who came to me said he would show me his dog—then he began to bark.
The Actor barks. The Entrepreneur's Wife seeks to calm him.
ACTOR: Another one said he was the best saxophone player in Carnegie Hall, shit on the floor and ate it up.
He kneels on the floor, pretending to eat off the floor.
ACTOR: Every three days I'd be confronted by the psychiatrist. He'd ask me "What's your name? Where do you live?" I live in the Bronx, I said. Washington Avenue and 449th Street. Always the same questions—what's your name, where do you

live— always the same.
Verena moves to the middle of the room, making quick dance movements.
SCHNEIDER: Verena!
ACTOR: (*crying*) The priest came to me and I didn't want to anymore, but he said to me to do it fast do it fast, we don't have much time, he said. (*screams*) I had a nervous breakdown for the whole fucking world!
VERENA: (*to Actor*) Would you like to dance with me?
ACTOR: I own nothing and allow everything. I give myself away. This ring—which is dear to me—the first person I see who needs it, take it it's yours.
He kneels in front of Verena, holding the ring out to her.
SCHNEIDER: Verena, I beg you—stop this minute.
VERENA: Would you like to dance with me, Gustave?
She curtsies. An embarrassed atmosphere comes over the guests. All watch Verena.
VERENA: Or you, perhaps, if I may ask?
She curtsies before the Producer. The Actor moves away.
ACTOR: (*on the way to the anteroom*) I looked people in the face, hoping they would look in mine and see my craft, my art— why doesn't anyone see me?
VERENA: (*curtsying to MP*) Would you like to dance with me?
SCHNEIDER: You'll have to excuse my wife, she's not feeling well right now—Verena!
VERENA: (*curtsying to Entrepreneur*) And you? Would you dance with me?
ENTREPRENEUR: (*with a tortured smile*) Thank you—Frankly, I don't dance.
Verena drapes herself around the Writer's neck.
VERENA: O Great Poet, you'll dance with me, won't you? I'll let you put your head between my legs if you do. Mommy will hold you then, OK?
The Writer at first embraces her softly, then, abruptly, pushes her away.
VERENA: Doesn't anyone want to dance with me?
Embarrassed silence.
ENTREPRENEUR'S WIFE: I think it would be important for her if you would establish a project of your own. For example, I built this society for aid to refugees, people nobody gives a damn about. You might even say I discovered a hole in the market. We're taking care of a group—Cambodian refugees who came to

Thailand. They're mostly dependents of the civil servants from the former regime—charming folks who weren't content to allow Pol Pot or some communist to take power in Cambodia. They're more for a democratic state where majority rules. They want political parties and not some red dictatorship.

VERENA: (*to Heiner*) Heiner, come over here and dance with your stepmother, please.

Verena takes Heiner by the hand and pulls him out in the middle of the floor.

VERENA: (*holding Heiner close and leading him in a couple of dance steps*) Do you know that it's not hard at all to make a woman happy? We expect so little from men. C'mon, try a little. We like it when men look us in the eyes when they talk to us. Don't have anything else on your mind when you tell us you love us. Hold me at the waist and turn with me, you need to be weak and strong at the same time, weak from work, but strong in bed. We want to lie in your arms and not feel like prisoners . . . .

She bends down from the back and falls on the floor. Heiner goes quickly to one side. The Entrepreneur's Wife goes over to Verena.

ENTREPRENEUR'S WIFE: (*helping Verena up*) Have you hurt yourself?

VERENA: Please come with me and let's get out of here. Let's go into town. Please.

ENTREPRENEUR'S WIFE: (*Looks at her husband and nods.*) OK.

The two women move to the anteroom.

VERENA: (*to the Producer's Wife*) Wouldn't you like to come with us too?

The Producer's Wife takes her husband's hand, he pushes it away.

PRODUCER: Go on then, go. When I say you can go—well, go.

The Producer's Wife goes along hesitatingly. The three women exit. The men stand in the room silently.

A Filipino goes to Schneider, smiling and shakes his hand.

FILIPINO: Thank you very much for this nice evening. I think we must go.

SCHNEIDER: You enjoyed it?

FILIPINO: Oh, it was lovely.

Blackout—Music.

Scene Six

Three hours later, same room. It is now approximately 3:00 A.M. From the garden one hears the first morning sounds from the nearby city. Heiner sits on the couch under the stairs. He still listens to his small cassette recorder through earphones. Gustave Schneider, the Member of Parliament, the Writer, the Entrepreneur and the Producer sit in easychairs. There has obviously been much drinking.
Silence.

MP: (*to the Writer*) In the village where I have my vacation home the farmers get up at 4:00 A.M. to go to Mass—by the time they get up and dress themselves it's just beginning to get light. The Mass is always the same time but today when they get up and go out it's still completely dark. They're the same farmers—they used to be young, now they're old. Within one generation things have gotten a bit darker—there's so much stuff in the air that no light comes through, you understand? Everything has gotten darker.

The Writer does not react.

MP: (*talking to himself*) . . . you just gotta check out of this . . . Apocalypse—you know that's a word I use so seldom, it's hard for me to even say it . . . Apocalypse.

He laughs. Silence. Schneider stands up, goes to the anteroom and returns.

SCHNEIDER: Where are those women? This is ridiculous.

Silence.

SCHNEIDER: (*to MP*) Can you imagine it? An acquaintance of mine—a very beautiful woman suffered from a kind of traumatic brain injury caused by an automobile accident. She was on the road to recovery but suddenly, because she had been lying down for so long and for other reasons a thrombosis formed in her head and she became psychologically impaired. She lay there with all this expensive and shiny apparatus when all of a sudden she began to eat her own vomit; she began to eat her own vomit. There's just nothing you can do about it.

Silence.

SCHNEIDER: I can't bear abnormality any longer.
Silence.
MP: (*talking to himself*) The work in committee, the so-called speeches—good for nothing. Everything's already been decided and everyone knows how things will turn out.
Silence.
MP: And in committee we talk but about what? The plans of the minister—there's never anything else to discuss. The man informs us of the latest with the Arabs and Palestinians. The various ministers regale us with their plans and tell us what laws are coming up and how we should vote on them.
Silence. The Writer, sitting in front of his recorder, takes a candle, lights it and holds his hand over the flame.
MP: Once I tried to do something—just once, but never again. I made the suggestion we should meet with the ministers without any agenda; that we should just talk about things we felt were really important. Only one cabinet minister thought that was a good idea and invited us to get together. He picked an old run-down restaurant in the country. We had a great meal and even better wine. A gypsy band supplied the music. We were all relaxed and in a good mood but we never got to talk about the problems. We never got a chance, not a chance.
The Writer cries out.
SCHNEIDER: Are you crazy? What are you doing?
WRITER: I would like to know where the women are. They can't have been in town all this time.
ENTREPRENEUR: (*to Schneider*) There's a real worker shortage in town. For example, in my line of work—construction—a big shortage. That kind of problem leads inevitably to a bad work atmosphere, low morale. If we build this clinic of yours then I need some gung-ho workers, not the deadbeats who hang around town but guys from the country who really know the value of a steady job. A job shortage strengthens morale—up to a certain point, that is.
SCHNEIDER: (*to Writer*) If a man has a few extracurricular activities, women destroy you and that's the truth.
WRITER: I am not I.
    In free verse.
    In search of myself

I will pull out my hair
Smash my skull
Tear down my limbs
And cut open my chest.
At the end of all this
There will lie before me
A pile of flesh and bones
About one foot high
And I will still not be myself.

The Writer stands up and goes to the buffet table and takes a knife. He begins to cut away the buttons on his shirt.

ENTREPRENEUR: (*to Schneider, pointing to the Writer*) Would you ask him to stop that.

SCHNEIDER: (*screams at him*) Hey, cut that out!

The Writer drops the knife and laughs hysterically. The Entrepreneur takes a plate and begins to eat.

ENTREPRENEUR: I admit I really feel no need to be somewhere where big is happening. Things are always popping up that don't fit into the plan. (*to Schneider*) Tell him to stop it, it's all cleaned up. I've spent my entire life trying to keep things straight.

PRODUCER: (*gazing off into space*) Besides me, someone sits who observes me—namely, me. Next to him sits someone observing him—that's me again. And next to him someone's sitting keeping watch—and on and on—one is always watching the other.

ENTREPRENEUR: (*woefully*) I know there are certain emotional outpourings which might indeed be necessary. But you never know how things will turn out.

MP: Natural, it's all natural. We've been tripping over our own enlightened doctrines for thousands of years, but the bestial face of man is always there, stepping out of the darkness.

He spills a glass of wine.

MP: That's the world according to Robert Michels but no one's listening. Every society has its oligarchy, even democratic society. Hey, do you have any spot remover?

Silence. The MP desperately tries to clean up his pants with a handkerchief.

ENTREPRENEUR: (*lightheartedly*) Do you have any porno films?

Silence.

PRODUCER: No eyeball, no bone, nothing we use to talk with, smell with, breathe with, speak with, kiss with, taste with, you can ever buy, nothing that's bent can be made straight. The really important things in life are not to be bought and that's really the righteousness of God. Real life can't be bought—look around you here—the garden, trees, mountains, air, earth—it can't be bought. Where's that fat Yugoslav who's been around all night?

SCHNEIDER: You mean Draga?

PRODUCER: Draga is that child's name. Go get her to come down.
Schneider glances toward the anteroom, then calls up to the first floor.

SCHNEIDER: Draga!

PRODUCER: One must reach out to these minorities.
Schneider goes up stairs. All eyes follow him up.

PRODUCER: I believe in the power of sin. In Religion class my teacher would ask to rank the sixth commandment—first, second, third? Sixth, of course, in other words farther down the ladder. Where is that Draga—everything that serves the cause of life must be supported.
Silence. The men look to the upstairs.

ENTREPRENEUR: As stupid as it may sound, you know it's tenser here than in the Eastern Bloc.
Silence. Schneider and Draga appear on the steps; he holds her hand. Draga appears sleepy, she wears a nightgown.

DRAGA: (*with accent*) What is the matter?

PRODUCER: Tell her that we have nothing against Yugoslavs—quite the contrary, in fact. We only have something against people who don't follow their natural inclinations. Tell her that the existence of evil is necessary—otherwise Goethe's Faust would be all the more boring without Mephisto.
All laugh. Schneider leads Draga down the stairs.

SCHNEIDER: There's no need to be afraid—he was just joking.

PRODUCER: Gentle Miss may I ask that you take my arm and walk a bit with me? Now Draga you have to say—I'm no miss and no gentlelady, I can climb the stairs alone. Say it in Yugoslavian, if you want.
Draga stands in the living room—the men surround her. The Writer remains sitting in front of his recorder.

MP: Allow me!

He takes Draga's hand, kisses it gallantly and then his kiss changes into dog-like licking. Draga pulls her hand away. The MP wipes off his mouth with his handkerchief.
MP: According to Robert Michels, the most important idea is the drive for status. He's convinced that this drive is even more forceful than even our sex drive—with which it is indeed closely connected. Women satisfy their need for status by choosing a man of influence. And men, accordingly, use their status to attract appropriate women—it's all in our nature.
Silence. The men and Draga look at each other. The Producer gently lifts Draga's nightgown.
PRODUCER: You have to sin bravely, decently—you can't be a timid hesitater.
Draga pushes him away.
SCHNEIDER: Don't be a killjoy, Draga.
Silence. The Entrepreneur positions himself quite closely in front of Draga.
ENTREPRENEUR: How much?
Silence.
DRAGA: One thousand schillings or I go back to bed.
ENTREPRENEUR: Thank you very much, I pass.
The Entrepreneur moves to the buffet table.
SCHNEIDER: It's alright, Draga, see you tomorrow.
DRAGA: Not tomorrow—now.
Schneider looks at the MP and the Producer. Then he pulls out his wallet and, unwillingly, gives her money. Draga moves to the buffet table, and takes a bottle of mineral water—she rinses out her mouth and then spits out the water on the floor.
DRAGA: Where?
PRODUCER: For him who loves everything becomes worthy, especially for him who loves God.
He takes Draga's hand and pulls her behind the couch. Schneider continues to look in the direction of the anteroom. The MP undresses down to his underwear, placing his clothes carefully over a chair. The Entrepreneur sits at the buffet table and eats from several trays simultaneously. The Writer sits in front of the recorder and stares into space.
MP: (*to Schneider*) Where is the bathroom?
Schneider points to a door next to the anteroom. The MP disappears into the bathroom.

ENTREPRENEUR: (*to Writer*) I married well, pay six thousand for a whore on the beltway—that's enough. I'm not crazy. My wife takes an active part in all that I do. I've rewarded her by giving her half of the firm.
The Entrepreneur eats. The Writer gazes off into space.
ENTREPRENEUR: All matters of importance to the firm are discussed at home—that is, every action we take we try to arrive at a consensus that satisfies us both. I don't need a smart-aleck woman if I want to have some fun—that only makes me more insecure. My wife and I have entered into a business venture, that's the only thing you can call it, really. She offers me her loyalty and interest in the business, I give her lifelong support. A woman over forty really doesn't have any other choice—she can't find work, so she has to take what her good husband has to offer.
The MP comes out of the bathroom and disappears behind the couch. Laughter is heard from behind the couch. Schneider goes to the stereo set and puts on a cassette of classical music. He looks to the anteroom and goes behind the couch.
WRITER: (*gazing off into the distance*) I am so useless—I can't do anything. All I can do is think of sentences—just sentences all the time. When they take away the cultural edges off our epoch the only thing left will be greed. We've banned prisoners to the basement of our society, and bring them out only when needed. I could hold an amazing lecture about the exploitation of the Third World—talk, talk, talk.
He rewinds the recorder, then fast forwards the tape. He stops the tape at various places, pausing now and then to rewind.
TAPE: " . . . I regard myself as a Socialist in the sense . . . Draga has a bladder infection . . . Who am I? Who am I? . . . The relationship is important to me . . . the Philippine Ambassador's son has a stomach-ache . . . in free verse . . ."
The Writer turns the volume louder. Heiner, who has been sitting unmoved beneath the stairs during the whole scene begins to move his upper body back and forth. The MP emerges from behind the couch and goes into the bathroom again. Schneider continues to look towards the anteroom, he is completely dressed.
TAPE: " . . . the world is ridiculous. The practice of medicine . . . physicians are butchers . . . I have cancer . . . a race of

fratricides . . . so-called Jew's Academy . . . petty bourgeois Christian-Socialists . . . limping souls . . . from the public library right into the concentration camps . . . no comforting shadow anywhere . . . union jargon . . . business jargon . . . jargon jargon . . . golden masks during the day and blubber helplessly at night . . ."
The MP comes from the bathroom and disappears behind the couch.
TAPE: " . . . Goebbels' friends . . . when can we eat . . . I really do love her . . . Public health has murdered the private sector . . . uterus . . . gallbladder . . . but you know that's off the record . . . source of income like any other . . . Daisy has— then for me at least the evening is saved . . . that I have feelings too, that I'm sensitive too . . . live on an island, swim in the sea . . . cancer is just a trade mark . . . up to eight hundred percent . . . covered with grime, blood everywhere, the defeat with my son . . . I am satisfied if I can work and earn money . . . financially, she's dependent on me . . . sure, completely helpless in everything . . . will be our going-away party, original . . . wonderful my dear . . . a woman, a princess . . . singing, celebrating a long laster . . . stopping family research, eh? . . . Hitler has been resurrected in the quiet suburbs . . . tagliabelle verde . . . in the champagne bracket . . . major criminal Franz Strauss . . . ."
The Writer continues to turn up the volume. The Entrepreneur becomes more and more involved in eating; Heiner moves his upper body more quickly back and forth. Behind the couch shriller noises are heard.
TAPE: " . . . How is your lovely child . . . a strict Catholic father . . . I am the devil, I am the devil . . . everything has become unbelievable—I can bind the capital investors . . . something doesn't fit. . . no alternative . . . life is guilt . . . the financing of the clinic for the terminally ill . . . is filled with tears and joy . . . I threw popcorn . . . am called Master, Doctor, too . . . I was my mother's one great love . . . I've become Christ . . . Rudolph Valentino, my father . . . Don't worry about . . . might not be any communism left . . . hurry up, we don't have much time, why doesn't anyone see me . . . in our generation things have become much gloomier . . . I am not I . . ."

WRITER: I can't live! I can't live! I can't live!
He tears out the tape, smashing it beneath its feet. Draga, on all fours, crawls out from behind the couch. She is wearing her nightgown and seems quite distracted. The Producer straddles her. He wears a shirt and tie and jacket, although no pants.
PRODUCER: (*shouting*) Long live the resurrection of the renaissance! Poor and rich, top and bottom, strong and weak—it's the systole and diastole of life!
Schneider and the MP peer from behind the couch and laugh. Schneider is completely dressed, the MP naked. Verena, the Entrepreneur's Wife, and the Producer's Wife enter the living room through the anteroom. The Writer approaches Verena.
WRITER: (*whining*) The play! The play!
He kneels before her, bending his head into her lap; she pushes him away.
The Producer's Wife stares at her husband, who still straddles Draga's back. The Producer falls, and on all fours, scurries away from his wife. She runs after him, swatting him severely on the rear.

Blackout—music.

Scene Seven

A half-hour later—same room. In the garden one notices the gradual morning light, one hears the birds and the sounds of the nearby awakening city. Heiner sits, inwardly collapsed, on the couch beneath the stairs. He still wears earphones.

Silence. Heiner does not move. Time passes.

Suddenly from a room upstairs, Verena and Gustave Schneider are heard arguing—no sentences, first screams, crashes, and objects breaking. Sobs. As suddenly as it began, it ceases. Silence.

The Elder Schneider in his wheelchair comes out of the garden into the living room. He looks about, then goes to the buffet table. He does not see Heiner. He takes a bottle of wine and pours himself a glass. He drinks the wine in one gulp—then belches.

ELDER: It's lovely when you can experience your own dying. That crazy monk Martin Luther—a genial pig-head, but a talented kid, too—said once that even if he knew that the world was going to end tomorrow, he would still plant his garden today . . . . You know, working in the garden gives meaning to life.
He pours himself another glass. From the upstairs room, more sounds are heard; objects falling against a door, sobbing. The Elder Schneider looks in the direction of the noise, raises his glass.
ELDER: To the living—from the young suicide victim Werther right up to those lifelong murderers. Werther was no love story—they're wrong—it's a great political drama of a rightless citizen who was kicked out of high society, regarded as dirt. Young Bonaparte, the revolutionary general, carries the book in his knapsack all the way to the pyramids—the Polish revolutionaries, the Spanish, the Hungarian—all understood Werther—they ran through the countryside, their torches burning bright—with the blood of the young murdered self-

inflicted deaths of the people—The great indictment of their rotten society was written in their blood. Today, too, in the streets of Berlin—a bicycle, a pair of shoes, blood spatters, the press applauds, death in the bathtub, the most virtuous, the bravest have gone under—and what's left? The money-grubbing crowds—Prost!
He drinks his wine in one gulp, pours himself another glass. The argument upstairs has ceased abruptly.

ELDER: Sleep no longer keeps the pain away from me nor does it keep the great horror from them.
He drinks up the wine, pours himself a new drink.

ELDER: To the children of insanity who put their fingers on the hot-plate, who invent the A-bomb and shout out how much fun it all has been. God has wrecked on the shore of science . . . in the twelfth century they declared theology to be a science—a devil's art—to grasp God, to put God in a full-Nelson. And there he sits—caught—behind barbed wire and smashed declarations and he's dying. The theologians have killed God—you can prove it.
He drinks the glass in one gulp.

ELDER: The beauty of it all is that I can take care of everything in my head and then dissolve the whole business and not feel a thing.
He turns the wheelchair around and gazes into the garden.

ELDER: The cities are getting tighter—until eventually you can't tell the seasons anymore, day, night, light and dark are all that's left. The Future—quite different is already inside me. From now on I don't intend to bother me or my enemies . . . the last worries, the last hopes . . . is tomorrow a day? Still day . . . is tomorrow still a day?
He moves into the garden. Silence. Heiner sits—caved inward—on the couch. The sounds from the room upstairs begin again and then end quickly. Silence. Time passes. Heiner does not move.

Blackout—Music.

Scene Eight

Six hours later—the same room. It is approximately 11 o'clock in the morning. Outside the sun is shining. The living room has been cleaned up. In place of the evening's buffet table one sees a morning breakfast table. Verena and Gustave Schneider are sitting at the breakfast table. Schneider reads the paper. Silence.

VERENA: Would you give me part of the paper, please?
Schneider gives her part of the paper. Verena stands up, takes an ornate vase from one of the small tables and wraps it in the newspaper. Schneider watches her. Verena returns to breakfast.
SCHNEIDER: Excuse me, but don't you find that a little irrational?
VERENA: Some of the dishes belong to me, too.
Draga enters the living room with a tray. Schneider and Verena sit silently. Draga sets the table—for four persons. She returns to the kitchen. Silence.
SCHNEIDER: Where's Dad? When it comes to eating, he's usually not far away.
VERENA: I want the savings passbook.
SCHNEIDER: The savings account is in my name. For all I care you can have the savings bonds—but only the ones that are already due—otherwise, we'll lose too much interest.
VERENA: And half of the furniture.
SCHNEIDER: Out of the question.
Draga comes from the kitchen; she brings coffee, tea and toast. Verena and Schneider sit silently. Draga serves them.
SCHNEIDER: Draga, would you get my son here for breakfast.
Silence. Draga goes back into the kitchen.
VERENA: The antique cupboard in the bedroom was my mother's—you know that, of course.
Schneider stands up, opens the lower drawer of the stereo set. A television is seen. Schneider switches the television on.
SCHNEIDER: The news is on—would it bother you if I watched it for awhile?
He returns to the breakfast table and looks toward the television set.

Silence.

VERENA: Whatever happened to the money my father lent me to put into helping your practice get started?

SCHNEIDER: Any other request? May I help you finance your future rounds at the bar?

Silence. Verena looks at Schneider.

VERENA: You're such a stupid pig.

SCHNEIDER: Thank you.

Draga comes out from the kitchen. Verena and Schneider sit silently. Draga serves soft-boiled eggs, bacon, etc.

SCHNEIDER: (*to Draga*) Go upstairs and get my son. Ask him if he would like a written invitation to come to breakfast.

Draga goes upstairs.

VERENA: Listen—I'm going to get the most expensive lawyer I can find—and ruin you.

SCHNEIDER: I imagine that you won't be able to get as expensive a lawyer as I can afford.

Silence.

SCHNEIDER: Tea or coffee?

Draga appears at the top of the stairs. She is upset. In one hand she holds the portable cassette recorder; with the other hand she makes the hangman's sign.

Schneider jumps up, a cup falls on the floor. He picks it up without thinking and runs up the stairs into the room. Verena follows him.

Draga comes down the stairs into the living room. She goes to the breakfast table, placing the cassette recorder and earphones on the table. She gazes absently at the breakfast table; she takes a piece of toast, spreads it with marmalade and takes a bite of the toast. From the room upstairs cries and sobbing can be heard.

The Elder Schneider in his wheelchair enters from the garden.

ELDER: (*to Draga*) What's going on in this house? Haven't they shouted enough at each other?

Draga swallows the toast.

DRAGA: The boy . . . Heiner . . . hanged himself.

Gustave Schneider appears at the top of the stairs. He pulls the lifeless corpse of his son down the steps into the living room. Verena follows. Music begins. The stage darkens slowly.

END

The Slackers

Dramatis Personae

Jack (Hans), 29, Steelworker
Diane (Anna), 26, Unskilled Worker, Jack's Wife
Schmelzer, 59, Steelworker
"The Italian," 42, Steelworker
Ringo, 22, Steelworker
Ursus, 35, Steelworker
Shakespeare, 61, Steel mill Librarian
Steward, 33
Waitress, 30
Personnel Manager, 36 (Female)
Personnel Manager, 48 (Male)
Worker, 34
Yugoslav, 40
Man
An American Singer (Female)
Minister For Labor And Commerce
His Wife
Quizmaster with His Two Assistants

Scene 1

An empty stage. William Shakespeare enters. He is an elderly man, dressed in a suit and appears rather unkempt. He is tipsy— as always. He drinks up a bottle of beer, then breaks the bottle over his head. He laughs.

SHAKESPEARE: I'm all right, Jack
How 'bout you?
My name is Shakespeare,
William Shakespeare.
Waitress, another beer!
WAITRESS: (*from off-stage*) Yessir, Mr. Shakespeare.
SHAKESPEARE: Forty years ago
The entire civilized world
Collapsed around me.
My life was a steel mill:
A huge conglomeration of iron.
And while everyone else
Died of injuries sustained
Somehow they managed to patch me up.
Civilization expired
But I returned to work,
I was quite a case.
Waitress, another beer!
WAITRESS: (*from off-stage*) Yessir, Mr. Shakespeare.
SHAKESPEARE: They discarded the worst pieces
And sewed my skull back together:
Bits of shell from the yoke
Ganglia stuck back to ganglia
Good as new, you know—
But not without a medical Miracle.
Then they covered up the job,
Namely, my head,
With a silver plate.
Wished me all the best
For the future.
Waitress—another beer!
WAITRESS: (*from off-stage*) Mr. Shakespeare,
Your beer is on its way!

SHAKESPEARE: Then, when I could talk again,
Babble is more like it,
They gave me a job as an
Assistant librarian.
I visited Stratford-upon-Avon
Forgot about Weimar
And mutinied on the Bounty
I hid among the Seven Swarves
And from my hideaway
Watched the rebirth of our
Domestic Steel Industry.

Waitress enters. She holds a bottle of beer in one hand, broom and dust pan in the other.

WAITRESS: Your beer, Mr. Shakespeare.
SHAKESPEARE: Keeper of the pearly gates,
St. Peter, will pick up the tab
Or, maybe, Father Schoenborn
Or, maybe, Sister Theresa
Or, maybe, the union's
Emergency Fund.
WAITRESS: Sure.
Mr. Shakespeare,
Are you going to smash the bottle
Over your head now
Or should I wait to sweep up the pieces
Until later?

Shakespeare takes a drink from the bottle. The waitress sweeps up the pieces.

SHAKESPEARE: She's a child of the mountains
Grown deaf
Amid the din and roar
Of the Canteens of Industry

Shakespeare takes a long drink from the beer bottle.

SHAKESPEARE: The great fire was over
The world had no longer
Its comfortable shadow.
The residue of the gas chambers
Burned in the eyes of the guilty
But they—they
Gazed into the future

Hungry for great deeds.
They ignited a new furnace:
Steel. Steel. Steel.
As if there weren't enough of them
On earth already
And among humankind.
They fueled the furnace
With the ruins of war:
Bullets
Grenades
Twisted moorings
A new blaze
Consumed the old.
In 1947
The new conflict
Ate up the war of reconstruction
Devoured its first flesh.
A furnace exploded.
The molten, glowing iron
Burned itself up from above
With the bodies of its servants
My brain is red-hot—
Waitress, another beer!

WAITRESS: There's still beer in that bottle,
Mr Shakespeare.

Shakespeare breaks another bottle on his head, beer runs down over his face.

SHAKESPEARE: These alcoholic drops
Fall like tears of the forgotten.
Waitress!
Where's my beer!

WAITRESS: For a poet
You're a real cut-up,
Mr. Shakespeare!

SHAKESPEARE: Is this the face
That launched a thousand ships
And burned the topless towers of Ilium?
Now she's s'posed to say,
Goodnight, sweet prince,
Let's go out for a drink.

Waitress exits, shaking her head.
SHAKESPEARE: Out of a single furnace
　　　　　　　Many came—
　　　　　　　And new ones followed the dead,
　　　　　　　They came from the fields
　　　　　　　From surrounding valleys
　　　　　　　From mom and pop's front yard
　　　　　　　Armed with their homemade stew
　　　　　　　And good advice.
　　　　　　　The church bells
　　　　　　　Became work sirens
　　　　　　　The graveyard
　　　　　　　The stone benches
　　　　　　　Where they ate lunch.
　　　　　　　A union steward, their priest,
　　　　　　　Baptized their calloused palms.
　　　　　　　Waitress! My beer!
WAITRESS: *(from off-stage)* Your beer, Mr. Shakespeare,
　　　　　　Is on its way!
SHAKESPEARE: The seasons disappeared
　　　　　　　Sun and moon
　　　　　　　Sank with the rhythm of the shift change
　　　　　　　The smell of hay vanished
　　　　　　　And with it the birds as well.
　　　　　　　Only stillness and noise
　　　　　　　Only neon and night
　　　　　　　That became their world
　　　　　　　I've gotta get outta here.
Shakespeare turns around to urinate. Waitress enters; she brings more beer.
WAITRESS: What are you doing, Mr. Shakespeare?
SHAKESPEARE: I'm bemoaning
　　　　　　　The loss of nature
　　　　　　　The absence of sunrise
　　　　　　　The exodus of the birds
　　　　　　　The vanished path
　　　　　　　Along the edge of the field
　　　　　　　The lost land
　　　　　　　Beneath the feet of men.
WAITRESS: Thank God

It's gone,
Mr. Shakespeare.
Where I grew up
The walls were always damp
The work was hard
Food was bad
And every father
Looked longingly—
Too longingly
Toward his own daughter.

SHAKESPEARE: What a pig.

The waitress sweeps up pieces of shattered beer bottles. Shakespeare grabs at her from behind.

SHAKESPEARE: You left the farm
And went to the mill canteen
And hoped
Amid the smell of the grease
Among the stares of horny workers
You hoped for one thing:
Virginity proffered
For love eternal.

Shakespeare lays his hands on her rear-end; the waitress stands up abruptly.

WAITRESS: At your age,
Mr. Shakespeare,
Really!

SHAKESPEARE: Isn't old wine
The finest and most mature?
Isn't its taste
The highest ecstasy?

WAITRESS: Aren't you getting a bit carried away?

SHAKESPEARE: Where else can you get
Carried away
If not with words?

Waitress exits.

SHAKESPEARE: When carnal ecstasy
Becomes ridiculous
Words are all that's left.
It's so hot in here
And I warm no one now.

                I am only good for
                Crazy speeches.
    He takes a long drink from the bottle.
SHAKESPEARE: For a long while now
                I have been cast adrift
                From the shore of life.
                I beat on an ocean
                Of Books,
                In a boat or words.
                No marital strife upsets my keel
                No mill accident
                No restructuring program
                No layoffs.
                I lie with Rasputin
                Titillate the Czarina
                I stand with Nero
                And watch Rome burn
                An eternal fire
                Has left me cold.
                My insanity sleeps
                Well-ordered
                In my brain.
                Yet the Inferno
                Lies in the coal-yard
                Just beyond.
    He crashes a bottle against his head and laughs.
SHAKESPEARE: I'm all right, Jack
                How 'bout you?

Scene 2

Total darkness. Ear-splitting noise is heard in the depths of a steel mill. The noise becomes softer, more muffled. Then, out of the confusion, a clarinet improvisation.

Scene 3

In the break room of a steel mill. A table, a pair of chairs. At the ceiling corners of the room hang video cameras: one in each corner. Four steelworkers are in the room: Ringo, wearing a racing cap, improvises on the clarinet; Ursus, wearing a battered farmer's hat, has his thumbs, playfully, in a table vise; the "Italian," wearing a torn and singed hat of a Venetian gondolier. In front of him, on the table, are video cassettes; the Italian is telling a story to Ursus. Ursus, his thumbs in the vise, listens intently.

ITALIAN: It's a beautiful summer's day
A girl runs through a green meadow
Two deer stand at the forest's edge
The girl has blond hair
She wears a dress that you can almost
See through
You can see everything, almost
The girl's parents are poor but—clean
When she runs, the girl's breasts
Bounce up and down
The sun is setting—slowly
The deer go back into the forest
The girl runs
To the edge of the forest
A cuckoo sings out
Behind a big tree
A dark stranger hides
With a beard and piercing eyes.
The girl keeps getting closer
He opens his shirt . . .
. . . And his pants
Do you want to know
How the film ends?

Ringo plays the clarinet.

URSUS: Go on.
Go on.

ITALIAN: Keep turning the vise
Or that's the end of the story.

Ursus turns the vise a bit more; he groans.

ITALIAN: The girl
Reaches the edge of the forest
The dark stranger
With piercing eyes

                    Jumps out from behind a tree—
                    He steps into the girl's way
                    "Look," he says,
                    "I work at the steel mill,
                    Right by the big furnace.
                    My whole chest
                    Is covered with burn scars.
                    That comes from the burning slag
                    And what doesn't hit my chest
                    Falls down my pants
                    And lands here.
                    God, my dick looks like
                    A watering can."
URSUS: What does the man do to the girl?
ITALIAN: D'ya wanna know?
                    You'd like to know, wouldn't you?
                    Keep turning.
Ursus turns the handle of the vise; he groans.
ITALIAN: What does he do to her?
                    Everything.
                    From the front
                    From the back
                    On top
                    On the bottom.
Italian gives the cassette to the others. Ringo improvises on the clarinet.
ITALIAN: My friends,
                    First-class pornography.
URSUS: But then what?
                    What happens?
ITALIAN: Whatta ya mean—then what?
URSUS: Does he marry her?
ITALIAN: Keep turning.
Ursus turns the handle; he groans.
ITALIAN: He doesn't marry her.
                    She dies of pneumonia
                    Because she was always
                    Running around half-naked
                    Through the woods.
Ursus groans; the Italian laughs.

SCHMELZER: Enough.
ITALIAN: (*to Schmelzer*)
     She doesn't really die.
     She just gets real sick.
SCHMELZER: I said stop it
     That's enough.
URSUS: Schmelzer, please
     I don't have any money for films.
     You know, the pay cut.
ITALIAN: It's the whore
     He goes to a whore every Friday.
     He pays for everything
     She and her pimp want.
     She laughs
     The pimp laughs
     The jerk just looks at her
     Says nothing
     And pays for everything.
URSUS: She's not a whore.
     The guy with her
     Isn't a pimp, either
     He's her brother.
     And she doesn't laugh at me.
     Really, Schmelzer,
     She laughs 'cause she likes to laugh
     That's all.
Schmelzer goes over to Ursus; Ringo improvises on the clarinet. Schmelzer turns the handle of the vise slowly, and yet steadily. Ursus cries out in pain.
SCHMELZER: Haven't they laughed enough
     At you.
     They laugh at school
     Because you wet your pants
     Right in front of the teacher.
     They laugh at home
     Because you brought flowers to a pregnant cow.
     Your brothers and sisters laugh at you
     Because they disinherited you
     And divided up your part of the spoils.
     Haven't they laughed enough

At you?
URSUS: Schmelzer, Schmelzer.
SCHMELZER: That's enough laughing.
Schmelzer quickly opens the vise; Ursus falls into his arms.
Ringo plays a tune on the clarinet.
SCHMELZER: They can't do anything
To you around here—
You're a son to me.
The Steward enters. He wears a black coat. Suddenly, everything becomes quiet—even the clarinet.
STEWARD: Everything okay, guys?
There is no reaction to the question. Silence.
STEWARD: (*to the Italian*)
New porno, eh?
New horror?
No reaction. Silence.
STEWARD: Schmelzer
Why don't you talk to me?
Don't you know anything?
The Steward takes a few dance steps.
STEWARD: When I was still at the furnace
And the burning slag
Fell from the sky
Who got out of the way fastest?
Who made the quickest twists and turns?
I did—the dancer.
I was a son to you.
No reaction. Silence. The Steward dances a few steps.
STEWARD: You all used to laugh at me before.
Why not now?
No reaction. Silence.
STEWARD: Don't you see what's wrong here?
They've closed down the foundry
They've put the rolling mill on half-time
Sooner or later they'll
Put you all out in the street.
No reaction. Silence.
STEWARD: Where's Jack?
Why isn't he here?
He's in the Personnel Office

                    And whatta you think
                    They're telling him up there?
                    Sooner or later they'll put
                    You all out on the street.
                    That's what they're telling him
                    I know.
No reaction. Silence.
STEWARD: Schmelzer, I can fix it
                    So that you guys
                    Are the last to go.
No reaction. Silence.
STEWARD: The word from the boss—
                    If you guys don't start wearing
                    Safety hats
                    They'll dock your pay.
The Steward leaves. Silence.
SCHMELZER: How the hell can I see my sons
                    If I stand on the bridge
                    And only see a bunch of safety hats
                    In front of me?

Schmelzer goes to a corner of the room and talks to the video camera.

SCHMELZER: I gotta know
                    Who's who:
                    The green hat with the holes,
                    Now that's Ursus
                    The red-neck from the sticks.
                    The guy with the big heart and the strong arms.
                    If he's just wearing one of those
                    Safety hats
                    Ursus is not Ursus
                    He's just like anybody else.
                    But he's the only guy
                    Who can lift the iron trough
                    If there's a stoppage in the crane.
                    He can straighten out the slag rods
                    When they get bent up—
                    With his bare hands.

Schmelzer points to Ringo's racing cap. Again he speaks into the camera.

SCHMELZER: Ringo,
　　　　　　 Like my own son,
　　　　　　 The race-car driver.
　　　　　　 On payday he leaves them all behind.
RINGO: I'm sittin' in my car
　　　　 And all of a sudden
　　　　 We start to fly
　　　　 My car and me.
　　　　 We fly over everybody
　　　　 Over houses
　　　　 Over the earth
　　　　 Nothing and nobody can touch us.
SCHMELZER: A week's pay
　　　　　　 For speeding tickets.
　　　　　　 And on his day off
　　　　　　 He's Mr. Race-Car Man
　　　　　　 The King of Speed.
RINGO: Tell 'em
　　　　 That I'm the best clarinet player
　　　　 In the whole damn mill.
SCHMELZER: (*screams into the camera*)
　　　　　　 He's the best clarinet player
　　　　　　 In the whole damn mill.
RINGO: Tell 'em
　　　　 That I'll play real pretty
　　　　 At their funeral.
SCHMELZER: Play for 'em.

Ringo stands in front of the video camera. He looks into the camera. He looks over to Schmelzer. He looks back to the camera. He plays a funeral march. Schmelzer points to the Italian.

SCHMELZER: That's the Italian
　　　　　　 Our story-teller.
　　　　　　 His hat belonged
　　　　　　 To a Venetian gondolier.
　　　　　　 Tell 'em about it.

The Italian goes over to the video camera.

ITALIAN: Them?

He looks alternatively to Schmelzer and into the camera.

ITALIAN: I was in Venice on vacation.

I saw the most beautiful woman in the world.
She never would've fallen for a
Dirty steelworker like me.
But she climbed aboard
When a charming gondolier bowed deeply
Offering her his gondola.
I rented the whole thing:
Clothes.
Hat.
Even the gondola.
All from a real gondolier.
The most beautiful woman in the world
Was, in fact, a saleswoman
From the German Federal Republic.
I didn't say a word.
No story, no sentence, not a single
Syllable.
One word would've given me away.
But my arching eyebrows
My look
My embrace
My warm breath
That was Venetian enough
And I will always be for her
A Venetian Gondolier!

He screams into the video camera
You guys are shit!
You would've fallen out of the gondola
At the very idea of
Fucking a German saleswoman!

Schmelzer goes over to the camera.

SCHMELZER: My head is free
And it's gonna stay that way.
I need air
Between me and danger.
All the worst shit comes from above
And my head can smell it
So I get out of the way in time.
I've never been hit by any
Falling stars yet:

>   No degree from school
>   No praise from no boss
>   No wedding ring from no wife
>   Here in Hell
>   It's hot and my charcoal sons
>   Don't smell the shit anymore
>   But I do—I'm Schmelzer—
>   The guy with no hat.

He pulls down his pants and turns his rear-end toward the camera. The others do likewise. Jack, the fifth worker from the furnace group, enters the break room. Silence. Schmelzer goes over to him.

SCHMELZER: Jack
> So what did they want from you in Personnel?
> Jack!
> Say something.

Jack breaks into wild laughter.

Scene 4

In the living room of Jack and Diane's small home. Jack sits at the table, eating and drinking. He watches a pornographic video film. Now and then he operates the remote control—mostly fast forward. Occasionally he presses the "slow" button. He is silent. Diane gazes at him for a long time.

DIANE: What's the matter, Jack?
> Since you've been home
> You haven't said one word.
> If you close your eyes
> All the bad things go away
> And everything's okay again.
> Yesterday in the factory
> I closed my eyes
> And all of a sudden
> I was on a Caribbean cruise.
> Some rich fellow had invited me
> But he wasn't any good.
> Then a plain old sailor
> Smiled at me—he had honest eyes

And so I think to myself
That's the man for a lifetime.
And when I opened my eyes
There was a problem on the assembly line
A short somewhere, a fuse blown.
The boss said he was gonna dock my pay.
I always think these things
Even as a young girl
You close your eyes
When you walk through the woods
And that's when the elves appear.
Or maybe just a tour-guide
Who'll buy you a drink.
It's true, you know.
If you go to the Maldives
They give you a free drink—
Bacardi with Coca-Cola
From the leader of your tour.
Just once I'd like to see a real ocean.
If you get someone to subscribe
To the newspaper
You get a weekend for two
At the Holiday Inn.

Diane undresses. She wears "provocative" underwear.

DIANE: You know, really
We've got it pretty good.
We can go anywhere we want to.
All that's missing is the furniture
For the baby's room
. . . And the baby.

Diane makes a seductive gesture in front of Jack.

DIANE: If you take my salary
And my Christmas bonus
And my vacation pay
And add it to your pay
And your Christmas bonus
And your vacation pay
Then we can just about pay off
The baby's room in installments
As well as the video recorder.

Only, we can't afford
Any emergencies.
At the factory
They're laying off the women now.
Before they even work long enough
To qualify for unemployment.
The woman next to me was fired
Before the end of her third month.
For no reason at all:
She went to work in the morning like
Any other day and there it was
In red ink on her time card
It said they couldn't use her anymore.
The foremen weren't around.
So she went home and painted her
Living room red.
That won't happen to me
When I get pregnant.

She sits on top of him. Jack gazes over her shoulder at the pornographic film.

DIANE: Hold me tight
Close your eyes
And imagine me.

Jack does not react. Diane closes his eyes for him.

DIANE: D'you want me to be like her?
You know I can think of everything.
You just need to tell me
How you want to imagine me.

Jack does not react. Diane watches the film and tries to "act out" the film. She moves up and down; she imitates the dialogue of the film.

DIANE: Take me
With all your strength
Drill me
Extinguish me
I am your vessel
Fill me.

She speaks normally again.

DIANE: I've ordered the things for the baby's room.
Very cheap—and all wood.

For our child.
In the catalogue it says
That the prices will be going up.
You're not mad at me, are you?
Am I doing it right?
Is this the way you imagine it?
You know, I bought a conch shell—
You put it up to your ear
And you can hear the ocean.
See, you really don't have to
Actually *go* there
If you can't afford it.
I can feel you deep inside me.
They have one of those things at the store—
You shake it and it looks like snow's falling.
A village in the Alps
You go skiing in the winter
And then you drink
Bacardi and Coke in the Hotel bar.
I'm always thinking about stuff like that.
Can you touch me, just
Now and then?

William Shakespeare enters. He appears totally unkempt and is thoroughly drunk.

SHAKESPEARE: Thirst. Thirst. Thirst.
I have nothing to drink.
And you waste your life fucking.
The juice of Lust
Drips and oozes into the numberless
Houses by the mill—
I'm Falstaff on the wagon.
Captain Silver without his rum.
Your friends, er, colleagues
All enemies of literature, of art.
They drive me from their door.
Give me some money, Jack.
I'm dying of thirst.
Your heart is full of sand.
I crawl through the desert on all fours
I disturb your peace

I trample down your gardens, your carpets.
I interrupt your well-earned vacations.
I scream into your silences:
Why do you look at me
William Shakespeare
For forty years already
With the same expressionless
Expressions?
I have the treasures of the soul
At my disposal.
Why does no one approach me
And touch a book?
Your heart is a desert
The whole country is a desert
This dry look
Makes me infinitely thirsty.
Thirst. Thirst. Thirst.
Give me some money, Jack
I'm dying of thirst.

He lies down on the floor.

SHAKESPEARE: The death of the modern soul
Takes place on a working man's
Cheap wall-to-wall indoor-outdoor carpet.
Very well, I expire
Upon this easy-care
Synthetic rug.

Shakespeare "dies."

SHAKESPEARE: Death is a warning.
Therefore a final word:
With me go Ulysses
Marco Polo and Francis Drake.
They transformed the deserts of this world
Into the sea and the dry land.
Save them, Jack.
The death of these giants
Can still be prevented
With just a single bottle of beer—
How 'bout it?

Shakespeare "dies" a second time.

SHAKESPEARE: The truth is—

Nothing has really affected me.
No story no book
I turned to sand long ago
And now I crawl on all fours
Through my own desert.
I cry out into my own silence.
Save me, Jack.
Tonight I don't want me
To be the ruin
Of me.

Jack goes to his jacket, takes out his wallet. He gives Shakespeare money.

SHAKESPEARE: I sense the first drops
Of blessed rain.
I hear the crash of waves
On the distant shoreline.
Come, brother
The damp counter-top
Awaits us—A new domain
The bar is filled with wonder tonight
The Armada weighs anchor
At the bottom of a bottle.
Back to belles-lettres
Mesdames, Messieurs
I do hope my entrance upon the stage
Which now becomes my exit
Will not hinder your continued
Copulation.

Shakespeare exits. Diane gets dressed. The pornographic film continues. While Diane speaks, Jack slowly, but steadily, increases the volume.

DIANE: Why did you give him money, Jack?
He'll only come back for more.
Every night he'll stand around
And want money.
Why doesn't he go away from here
Why does he stay
The only one left in the rooming house
Because of him
They can't tear it down.

He could move to the projects
Or go away for good.
They've already tried to get him
Committed.
You can't hold up the process forever
Just because of him—
We're outta here, too, sooner or later,
Everyone's outta here.
Jack?

Jack does not react.

DIANE: You can depend on me Jack.
When I open my eyes
All I want from life
Is what everyone else wants.
You know:
That you can almost pay your bills
That no one loses his job
That I can have children.
I can't close my eyes
And you can't throw life away—
We've got
What we've got.
They can't take it away from us.
What's wrong, Jack?
Is everything okay?
Or at least, is something okay?

Jack does not react. Diane takes up the conch shell and examines it. She places the shell to her ear.

DIANE: It's hard to have no dreams
When you can hear the sea
So clearly.

Diane closes her eyes.

DIANE: The ship is already on the open sea
It's headed for the Maldives.

Jack stands, takes the conch shell from Diane and hurls it against the wall. The shell shatters. Diane erupts into a wild fit of laughter.

Scene 5

The personnel office of the steel mill. The Personnel Manager sits at her desk. The Steward, in a black coat, stands behind her. Jack stands in front of the desk. He appears nervous and confused. The Personnel Manager observes him closely.

MANAGER: You may speak now.
JACK: My name is Jack Freiberger
 They told me I'd be laid off
 There must be some kind of mistake
 I mean, it can't be true.
 My wife, Diane
 Has ordered everything for the baby's room.
MANAGER: Before you go any further
 Let's look at the big picture.
JACK: She wants to have a baby.
 A short, silent pause.
JACK: I was always a good worker.
 Check the records.
MANAGER: You have to look beyond
 Your personal situation.
JACK: The house.
 We're still paying on the house.
 We're still paying on a lot of things.
MANAGER: Let's look beyond
 Your personal situation.
 Let's look at the big picture.
 Think of Brazil, of Korea
 Or India—
 The steel mills in those places
 Are always expanding
 There's always more steel
 Coming out of the furnaces
 In those places.
JACK: I'm a good worker.
 Schmelzer trained me
 And everyone knows

He's the best.
MANAGER: They've got good workers, too
And they're getting better.
Soon they'll be the best.
Then they'll train new workers
And then more steel will hit the market
And then that will be the end.
JACK: The end?
MANAGER: The market.
Don't you understand?
JACK: Yes.
MANAGER: Then will you sign your release, please?
JACK: Why me?
MANAGER: It's nothing personal.
STEWARD: It's nothing personal.
MANAGER: It isn't your fault.
It's the market.
We have to cut our costs.
Tighten the belt
In Personnel.
JACK: In the rolling mill
There's a guy
Who's always goofing off.
MANAGER: You still don't get the big picture.
The lazy worker, the good worker
The fat and the thin
The rich and the poor
You and I all have
To draw the belt a little tighter.
When times are good
They're good for all.
When times are bad
Everyone must sacrifice—
Don't you agree?
JACK: Sure.
When the pay cuts came through
I told the guys that everyone
Had to give a little.
And when our Christmas bonuses
Were cancelled

>   I told them, hey
>   We all take it on the chin
>   In this business.
>   And when things kept getting worse
>   They had to get worse for us, too.
>   I talked to the guys
>   Like you're talking to me now:
>   Straight talk
>   Like it is.
> *Jack becomes increasingly confident.*
> MANAGER: You are an intelligent man.
> JACK: And when they said
>   Layoffs were next
>   I didn't get too excited.
>   Some of us got real excited
>   But I don't need to name names.
>   And sometimes I think a little hard times
>   Might do some of these guys good
>   Just so that they can see
>   That things can't go on like this
>   Forever.
>   I even went to night school for awhile.
>   And three months ago
>   I got promoted from second assistant
>   To first.
>   When the chips are down
>   You can count on me.
> MANAGER: You are a very good man.
> JACK: I always say
>   The cream rises to the top.
> MANAGER: The world is your oyster.
> *She holds the release form and pen out for Jack to take. Jack is visibly irritated.*
> STEWARD: Sign, please.
> JACK: Steward, you know me.
>   Tell her that I'm the one
>   Who always gets the highest rating
>   In every evaluation.
> MANAGER: We're fully aware of that.
>   We depend on you

156 *The Slackers*

              And when the work goes
              You won't end up doing nothing
              You won't do anything
              Inappropriate.
              You won't hang around bars or
              Become a burden to the state—
              You'll find work again somewhere
              Because you're an intelligent and able
              Individual.
              And you're flexible enough
              to bounce back from adversity.
JACK: I don't want to leave here.
              Diane, my wife,
              Has work here.
              In the appliance factory.
              She gets these ideas into her head, you know
              But when the chips are down
              You can count on her.
              Old Schmelzer is here, too.
              And the house.
              And Shakespeare, the drunk.
              And the things for the baby's room
              Have already been ordered.
              I can't sign.
MANAGER: No one really wants to make you sign.
              We just want to talk to you.
              And make you understand the way things are.
              Let's talk again about the market.
              The market is more important
              than any one individual.
              It doesn't seem to follow any laws—
              It has its own laws.
              It's like the stars in the sky
              And whatever any one person says
              About any other person named Diane
              Who gets ideas in her head
              Or about a drunk named Shakespeare
              Or about some furniture for a baby's room
              The market never takes notice—
              These things never touch it:

| | No appeals
| | No stories
| | No single destiny
| | Can change the paths of stars, right?
| | We must recognize that.
| | You must recognize that.
JACK: I've got nothing against the market
          I've got nothing against the stars
          There'll always be heaven and earth.
          I always say—Just be yourself
          Do your thing
          Well, and I live in this place
          And my job is making steel.

The Personnel Manager changes her tone of voice. She takes a bundle of bank notes out of a drawer and holds it out to Jack.

MANAGER: Listen. You've worked here ten years. Here's ten thousand—That's a thousand for every year. I don't have to do this, you know. We're trying to show you our good-will. If you sign your release form now, the money's yours. Who knows what things will look like next week.

She takes a bank note from the bundle and holds it out for Jack.

MANAGER: A thousand for the first year.
JACK: I came to this city
         From the sticks.
         My father had a cabinet shop
         In a small town.
         At night, and on Sunday,
         He always locked himself away
         In his workshop
         And carved wood by hand.
         But all the farmers wanted were water troughs
         For their pigs or closets for their
         Linen and dishes.
         I was a fat and happy kid.
         My father always chased us out of his shop—
         This is for work, he said, not for play.
         My mother used to say
         That soon we'd have no more work

Because he always made things
No one wanted.
In 1969
My father went to the bathroom
And my mother wondered where he was
Keeping himself for so long.
And she went to find him
And I went, too, and I saw
How my father had hanged himself
On the bathroom light fixture.
At the children's mass
I was an altar boy and I thought that
God, Jesus Christ and the four Evangelists
Had become my father.
You see, in case one died
There was always another one to take over.
The last time I went to confession
I was fifteen.
My older brother took over the shop
He switched over to formica counter tops
I went to work in the factory.
At first, it was really hard.

MANAGER: A thousand for the second year.
JACK: The guys always laughed
Because beer got me drunk fast.
I couldn't drink
Their "free" milk either.
MANAGER: A thousand for the third year.
JACK: Old Schmelzer always said
He'd wake up to the deal, too,
Someday.
MANAGER: A thousand for the fourth year.
JACK: The worst thing
Were the night shifts.
At midnight
When Schmelzer opened the doors
And the livery began to smoke
I'd get real tired.
I just wanted to fall into the furnace.
If you don't have a home

              I thought at least you'd be
              At home in there.
              Schmelzer sent me out to the gate
              And rubbed my face with snow.
              When I got back
              He grabbed me by the neck
              And held my head real close
              To the furnace
              Then he sent me out again.
              Hot—cold, always the same,
              Hot, cold.
              He used to say
              That if you couldn't tell the difference
              You were done for.
MANAGER: A thousand for the fifth year.
JACK: The Italian put a dead mouse
              In his sandwich once
              Then he said
              "You don't have a wife yet
              To make you a decent sandwich,
              Here, have a bite of mine."
              And when I bit into it
              They all broke up laughing.
              I kept the mouse in my mouth
              Until they stopped laughing.
              Three days later
              I welded the Italian's bike
              Onto a pole in the lot.
MANAGER: A thousand for the sixth year.
JACK: That was when I
              Was going with Iris.
              Iris was a waitress
              Diane worked with in the restaurant—
              In the kitchen—
              Every night I waited for closing time
              And I'd ask Iris if she'd
              Take me up to her room.
              When she'd say no
              I'd go somewhere 'n drink until morning
              Sometimes Diane would sit next to me

                And would tell me how bad Iris was.
                For Diane there are only good people
                And bad people.
                I'd be totally out of it
                By six o'clock when I packed
                Up for work.
                Schmelzer would take me
                To the break room
                And lay me on a bench
                And cover me up with a coat.
                When the shift foreman
                Did his rounds and asked about me
                Schmelzer said I was on the toilet—
                Diarrhea.
                The foreman would laugh
                And that was that.
                After six weeks of this business with Iris
                I asked Diane to marry me and so
                We got married.
                We started building a house right away
                In case she got pregnant.
                They gave us a good deal
                With the loan.
MANAGER: A thousand for the seventh year.
JACK: That's the year
                One of the guys got burned to death—
                I mean, Erwin.
MANAGER: A thousand for the eighth year.
JACK: They allowed me to put in the alloy
                By myself by then.
                And when the report from the lab came back—
                Schmelzer nearly killed me.
                He held the paper up in the air
                And shouted out—
                "Can you guys remember
                That fat red-neck
                Who wandered in here eight years ago?
                Looka this."
                The best results in months!
                It was like I won an election or something.

             I climbed up to the platform
             And everything gets real quiet, see.
             Like a political rally on TV:
             Spotlight on the candidate
             A reporter throws out a question
             The candidate says something important
             Lights everywhere and the crowd goes crazy!
MANAGER: A thousand for the ninth year.
JACK: Then I went to night school.
             After all, you really gotta
             Have that piece of paper—
             Without it, you're nothing.
MANAGER: A thousand for the tenth year.
JACK: I know the economy's not so good
             But I've made it to first assistant
             I'm doing okay.
MANAGER: Take the money.
             Sign the release form.
STEWARD: Go ahead, take it.
             Take and leave.
The Personnel Manager pushes the money into Jack's hand. Jack looks at the money. Silence.
MANAGER: I need a hundred and twenty
             Volunteer layoffs.
Silence. Jack looks at the money and shakes his head.
JACK: But I'm a good worker.
He throws the bills into the face of the Manager. The Steward watches and suppresses a laugh. The Manager is taken aback. She takes a whip from out a desk drawer. The scene changes into one from a horror film. During the following the manager strikes first Jack, then the Steward with her whip.
MANAGER: Why do you guys
             Stick to the blast furnace
             As if the dust were air
             And the heat food?
             You're just a mass of flesh and impotence
             You're insects consumed by the fires
             Of burning steel
             Your death stinks of burning flesh.
             I've known your faces

And their rubbery lines
Since I was a kid.
I grew up in the same towns
I came from the same type of families
I dragged a lunch-pail to the edge of fields—
Just like all of you.
And I drank from the same half-empty
Thermos mug—just like you, too.
Your jokes and cat-calls
Still stick to my skin.
I left the sticks for the big city
I cleaned the rich folks' shit
I took the abuse of the social workers
And the foster families—
I went to school
And I've had enough of your
Beer-drenched kisses and putrid cocks.
But I can't get away from your smell.
You multiply like animals
Your children crowd the Personnel Office
Like eager lambs led to slaughter.
Why don't you get out of here?
Why don't you get out of my life?

The Steward grabs at an iron letter-opener, which lies on the desk. The Manager grabs at it also, but in vain; the Steward is too quick, he scalps the Personnel Manager.

MANAGER: Help! Help!
JACK: Help! Help!
Diane, Schmelzer, Shakespeare!
Help me, I don't want to quit!

The horror-film atmosphere is over. The Personnel Manager is once again seated at her desk. The Steward places the letter opener on her desk and places himself behind the Manager. The Manager speaks with Jack in a matter-of-fact tone of voice. Blood runs down her face.

MANAGER: No one wants to lay you off.
We wish to speak with you
We wish to convince you
Let's talk again about the marketplace
The market is more important than

Any one individual
It follows its own laws—not ours
It's like the stars in the sky
Whatever men have tried to tell the stars
The stars don't listen, they can't hear.
We must remember that—
You must remember that.

Jack regards the bleeding Personnel Manager; he begins to laugh.

Scene 6

Shortly before noon, in the canteen of the steel mill. Video cameras hang from the ceiling. Jack sits at a table with a waitress. At a table next to him, William Shakespeare. Shakespeare is pale and shaky. He looks over to Jack repeatedly. Several tables stand in the foreground; they are covered with white linen table cloths. Underneath the table cloths one recognizes the outline of cold meat platters. Jack gazes into his beer. He is already somewhat drunk.

JACK:	Is the world unfair Or is the world not unfair?
WAITRESS:	Yeah, yeah.
JACK:	Am I a good worker Or am I not a good worker?
WAITRESS:	Yeah, yeah.
JACK:	And why does the shift foreman tell me— "Jack," he says "You haven't signed the release form. Do what you want Take a walk, get drunk Lie down in the hall Take a nap I can't give you any work. I can't put you on the list." Why?
WAITRESS:	You've been asking me that all morning.
JACK:	Why? Why can't he

	Put me on the list?
WAITRESS:	Why are you asking me?
	I didn't make the world
	No one asks me why I'm here.

Jack looks at the Waitress.

JACK: Why are you here?
WAITRESS: To listen to this.
You know, you guys
Always come here
And I sit here
Listening to you tell
Me how you owe so much money
Or that your wife doesn't understand you
And when I begin to fall for your line
You're busy Saturday night.
JACK: Diane, my wife
Has already ordered stuff for the baby's room.
She lost her job, too.
Because the appliance factory
Closed up and moved everything to Spain.
The only thing I know about Spain
Is that you take your vacation there.
What the hell do they know
About putting together washing machines?
WAITRESS: Another beer?
JACK: She doesn't have any work
I have a job
But I'm not allowed to work.
Is the world unfair or
Is the world not unfair?
Shakespeare, you drunken slob,
Come here.

Shakespeare moves to Jack's table and joins in on their conversation with a swiftness that one would hardly have thought possible.

JACK: When the dog's s'posed to talk
You can't get a word outta him.
He always has his mouth open for somethin'
Now it's closed, for Christ's sake.

Jack pushes a beer over to Shakespeare; Shakespeare drinks it in one gulp.

JACK: Why?
SHAKESPEARE: The world, the world
Please, Jack—
Another beer.
JACK: Another beer
For the gentleman.
WAITRESS: Jack, once you've started with him. . .
You need to keep your money for yourself.
JACK: I'll spend my money
The way I see fit
Waitress, another beer
For Mr. Shakespeare.

Waitress stands up and gets another beer.

JACK: Okay, Shakespeare
You've been sitting in libraries
Reading books
For forty years.
After you've drunk my beer
I want to know
Why the world is the way it is.

The waitress brings the beer. She places it in front of Shakespeare. He looks at the beer, but he does not touch it.

JACK: Drink.

Shakespeare takes the beer and sips it hesitantly.

JACK: I told you
To drink it.

Shakespeare drinks the beer. He looks at Jack. Silence.

JACK: Why?

Silence.

SHAKESPEARE: *(softly)* Thanks for the beer.

Old Schmelzer, the Italian and Ursus enter the canteen. They go over to Jack's table.

JACK: Schmelzer
They won't let me get to you
Tell them that you need me.
Tell them
That you can't work
Without your
First assistant
I waited for three hours

                    In front of the Hall
                    I pressed my ear
                    Up against the steel wall
                    Sometimes I even thought
                    I heard your voice.
The workers sit at Jack's table. The waitress gets them beers.
JACK: Schmelzer, do something
                    I can't bear it much longer.
Schmelzer is silent.
ITALIAN: (*to Jack*) Calm down
                    They've brought Ringo
                    Into the Personnel Office.
The waitress places several bottles of beer on the table. Shakespeare, in an unwatched moment, drinks from all of them. The Italian places two video cassettes on the table.
ITALIAN: New porno
                    New horror
                    If they keep it up
                    No one will be able
                    To afford these films.
                    They say there's a Yugoslav guy
                    Somewhere in town
                    Who makes cheap porno
                    He can't beat mine
                    Mine always has a story.
Ursus takes up a video cassette.
URSUS: What about this one?
ITALIAN: Read the title.
URSUS: "In my mistress's lap."
                    What's it about?
ITALIAN: Life and Death
                    You shithead
                    You idiot
                    Your mama's cunt
                    The black hole
                    Spit you out into the world
                    Your whole life long
                    You kneel before your neighbor
                    You kneel before your secretary
                    You kneel before the saleswoman

	You kneel before the persistent furnace
	You beg
	For a warm place to stay—
	And when you die . . .
URSUS:	I go to Heaven.
ITALIAN:	Don't act so Catholic
	You red-neck
	Heaven is the biggest
	Cunt there is.
	A horny burning hole
	From eternity to eternity
	Nothing but chicks and dicks
	Amen.

The Italian laughs. Ursus looks at him with great, big eyes.

URSUS:	I don't want
	To end up in
	My mistress's lap.
ITALIAN:	Why not?
URSUS:	I always thought
	It was too cold there
	Beside the blast furnace
	At the mill
	It's always nice and hot.

The Italian strikes Ursus in the head with the cassette and laughs. Ringo enters the canteen. All look over to him.

RINGO:	Nothing to it, folks.
	Nothing to it.
	I just made mincemeat of that pig
	Of a Personnel Manager.
	I told her
	When you go for your walk
	On Sunday
	Wait for me.
	I'll be there with a hot iron
	And beat your head in
	And if you haven't had enough
	By then
	I'll keep coming back
	Again and again.
	Number your bones

      I says to her
      So St. Peter will know
      How to put you back together.
      When Ringo's finished with you
      Your own dog won't recognize you.
  He throws three thousand dollars onto the table.
RINGO: Waitress, bring out your best.
      As much as the guys want
      I'm buyin'.
The workers stare speechlessly at the money. Silence.
SCHMELZER: (*softly*) Put your money away, Ringo.
  Silence.
RINGO: Shakespeare, eh?
      How much can you drink today?
      A case?
      Two cases?
SCHMELZER: (*screams*) Put the money away!
  Silence. Slowly, Ringo puts the money away. Suddenly, Ringo sits down on Schmelzer's lap and begins to cling to him.
RINGO: Schmelzer, help me.
      I don't want to leave you!
  The chair with Schmelzer and Ringo falls over. Schmelzer crawls on the floor; Ringo continues to cling to him.
SCHMELZER: Why do you take
      My young sons—
      One after the other—
      Away from me?
      Why don't you take
      This old has-been?
      You won't have to pay
      Me to sign the release form:
      No unemployment
      No severance pay
      I'll volunteer
      I'll go willingly
      Into the furnace.
      I've been burned out
      For a long time anyway.
      When my wife left me
      I gave up on promotions

>   I buried my fire
>   With the flames of the blast furnace.
>   When my son couldn't
>   Look at me anymore
>   I slept for six weeks
>   In the ashes and slag.
>   I didn't die
>   But I stopped living, though.
>   I'm the one branch
>   You can throw into the fire
>   Without a thought.
>   Take me.

Silence. Ringo's sobs are the only sound. Shakespeare drinks from the various bottles on the table.

SHAKESPEARE: You're not enough, Schmelzer
            The furnace is hungry
            Every hair it singes
            Every bit of skin sticking to the doors
            Only makes it hungrier
            It's time for the big casualty list
            It's time for a big meal now.

SCHMELZER: (*cries out*) Shut up, you dog
           We're still alive.

SHAKESPEARE: Pardon me, Mr. Schmelzer
            You are the Lord of Hellfire
            I am but your scribe.

Schmelzer goes to the front of the room and pulls the white linen from the food. Bottles of champagne, wine, beer, mineral water, sandwiches have been underneath and are now visible.

WAITRESS: (*cries out*) Schmelzer
         Get away
         That's for the reception tonight
         There's a meeting between
         The Trustees and Executive Board!

SCHMELZER: (*laughs*) That?
          That's the bread
          From our flesh
          The wine
          From our blood
          We won't be eaten anymore
          We'll devour ourselves.

Schmelzer opens a champagne bottle, pours the contents over his head. Ringo, Jack, Ursus, the Italian and Shakespeare—in attack formation—rush the table of hors d'oeuvres. They eat all they can get their hands on. The waitress watches the scene. The Steward enters the canteen.

STEWARD: (*shouting*) Have you all gone crazy?!
Stop it! Now!
If you don't stop it now
I'll call the police.
I'll report you
There'll be layoffs!

Ringo begins to sing, the others join in.

STEWARD: (*shouting*) I'll put everyone here on the list!

Ursus knocks the Steward to the floor with one blow. Shakespeare kneels on the Steward's chest.

SHAKESPEARE: And when everybody's
On the list
Whatta ya gonna do then?
The lists need names
Then the list-makers will go on the list.

Shakespeare pours beer over the Steward's head; the Steward throws off Shakespeare and stands up.

STEWARD: Schmelzer
They're forcing me
If I don't get enough names
On the list
They send me back down
I don't know who else
To put on anymore
I'm one of you.

The workers shout out the words to the song they sing. The Steward takes a bottle of wine and hurls it against the wall.

STEWARD: I am one of you.

He joins in the others' shouting. The waitress enters with bucket, mop and broom. The attempts to clean up the mess—in the middle of the chaos. Shakespeare stands beside Schmelzer and points to him.

SHAKESPEARE: Take a look, Jack
This is the world:
An impotent cry

A limb that falls in a ditch
A crushed egg.
Shakespeare smashes an egg on Schmelzer's head. Schmelzer pushes him away. Shakespeare climbs on a table. He screams into the shouts of the workers and points to them.

SHAKESPEARE: Pigs squeal
When they're put to slaughter
By the butchers
Yet their flesh is digested
Quietly in the belly of the bacon eater.
I recommend to you grumbling gents
The study of history
Who are you?
You only get angry every fifty years or so
You come with pitchforks and rifles
And wage war on the powers that be
And think it'll all be done by tomorrow
Who the hell are you?
Even when Paris was yours
Your brave new world
Sank away in the graveyard
At Pere Lachaise.
Who the hell are you?
You are the slaughtered swine of history
Only recently, homeowners, too.
You cling, patient fools,
To foreign soil—for what?
Who are you?
Even in the best of times
You're just the memory
Of a struggle gone astray
From the fires you leave smoldering
Only a scent of smoke.
(*he laughs*)
And who am I?
A fool who always knows
better
I use the pencil of a scribe
To chop into my own thin ice.

Shakespeare pours beer over the shouting group of men and laughs.

Scene 7

The living room of Jack and Diane's home. The two sit on the couch, watching a television quiz show. On the couch next to Diane, there is a large, cheap plastic doll. Diane is knitting a dress.

DIANE: I don't understand this
                How could I have my period again.
JACK: Be quiet.
DIANE: I am quiet, Jack.
                I'm always thinking
                About what we need to do
                So that we don't have to
                Give up our house.
                I read in a magazine
                Where it might be a
                Problem with the man.
                I mean, he might not have
                Enough sperm.
                With the money that we still have
                We might be able to pay off
                Part of the interest.
                Then, maybe the bank
                Will cancel the foreclosure . . .
                Couldn't you go to the doctor
                For a sperm count?
JACK: I told you to be quiet.
DIANE: I could keep cleaning houses
                Or maybe go into business
                There are companies, you know
                They hire you for three hours or a day
                Or even a week.
                You just have to be home
                And wait for the phone to ring.
JACK: Would you be quiet?!
DIANE: You can't do it
                Without a telephone
                Can you remember
                When I promised you

	That I was going into this
	With both eyes open?
	That I had no illusions?
	Well, I do still have—
	Illusions.
	I see the projects where we grew up.
	It was hot near the stove
	But cold by the window
	When the wind blew.
	My father always put his beer
	On the window sill
	And in the winter time
	It would freeze.
	When his people came to power
	He said
	No worker will ever have to drink
	Defrosted beer again.
	I don't want to go back
	To the projects.

JACK: You know,
You could be quiet for
Just a moment.

DIANE: The best thing to do
We close our eyes
And then no one can find us.

Diane closes her eyes. Jack pulls a thick wad of paper tickets out of his pocket.

JACK: Look.
Whatta ya think this is?

Diane looks at the tickets.

DIANE: What's that?

JACK: Lottery tickets.

Diane stands and moves to the sideboard; she takes out an envelope. The envelope is empty.

DIANE: The money.
That was our last money.

JACK: So when I say
Don't worry
I mean don't worry.
Two weeks ago it was sixteen million

Last week—twenty-three million
I've thought it all out.
The woman who sold it to me
Gets twenty thousand
So that she keeps quiet about it
When the notice arrives
I put on my work clothes
Take my lunch pail
Just like a normal work day.
I go to the lottery office
And pick up my millions.
Then I go to the Credit Office
At the Bank
And when the guy moans,
"Why haven't you answered
Our last three notices?"
I grab him by the collar
Pull him over the counter
And say, "Quiet, man,
Don't be so fresh
Or I'll send you back to reform school."
I ask what I owe
Even though I know exactly that
Ninety-eight thousand dollars and eighty-five cents
Is still outstanding on the note.
I slap down a one hundred thousand bill
On the counter (*they have those, you know*)
"Keep the change," I says
"Use it for the day-care center."
Then I buy the best suit I can find
Go into the best restaurant
And eat myself silly.
After that, I go to the drugstore
Buy a laxative
A really strong one
And swallow down the whole bottle
At once.
Then, I go over to the mill
And wait.
When I feel it start to work

>   I go up to the offices
>   Where the general manager is
>   And shit on his desk.
>   I shit
>   And shit
>   And shit
>   But that's not the end of it.
>   Then I go to the Personnel Office
>   And shit out what's left on
>   The Personnel Manager and her files.
>   Then I go into the Mill
>   Get Schmelzer
>   The Italian and Ursus from the blast furnace
>   I'll get Shakespeare, too,
>   Out of the library:
>   We go buy a big American car
>   With a trailer
>   Inside the trailer
>   Inside the trailer is a huge refrigerator
>   Shakespeare rides in the trailer
>   We get Ringo from the rifle range
>   Where he hangs out now
>   And off we go to the French Riviera!
>   When one of us gets thirsty
>   We stop
>   And Shakespeare brings us
>   Fancy drinks—cocktails!
>   "How much," I says
>   And when some foreigner starts yakkin'
>   About this or that
>   I stick a hundred dollar bill in his mouth
>   And tell him to shut up.

DIANE: Don't you want to go with me
           To the Maldives?
JACK: Sure
           The next time
           I'll go with you.

Jack takes a cigarette-lighter and holds his hand over the flame.

JACK: If they think

176 *The Slackers*

> They can get rid
> Of a guy who's
> Done what I've done
> Then they're in for a big surprise.
> I'll come back
> I'll show them all.

Jack cries out in anguish; Diane embraces him.

DIANE: Take me with you, Jack
Take me with you.

JACK: Only the strong survive.

The quizmaster, with his two assistants, comes into Jack and Diane's living room. The living room transforms into a glitzy Hollywood-type quiz-show set—the transformation and the following game show sequence occur in rapid pace.

QUIZMASTER: This is just the right setting for our game: "Six from Forty-five." Forty-five men need work, but only six can get jobs. Only the strong survive. We are now in the living room of our next contestants: Jack and Diane Freiberger. Jack was laid off unconditionally a few weeks ago because he tore up the canteen at the mill where he worked. Diane, his wife, lost her job when the factory she worked in pulled up stakes and moved south. Both Jack and Diane have a great deal of debt, of course, and the bank has already threatened foreclosure . . . These two are really down of their luck. But they want to pull themselves up by their bootstraps. A perfect couple for our game: "Six from Forty-five." Forty-five men need work, but only six can be hired. Our own Usche and Barbara will accompany Mrs. Freiberger behind the stage for awhile, while Jack, I can call you Jack can't I? You and I will begin the game. You know the rules for "Six from Forty-five"—don't you, Jack? I ask you a series of questions and you answer with a yes or no. If you say no, unfortunately you are out of the game. . . If you say yes, you remain in the running. After each yes answer you must slap yourself in the face not too hard, after all, it is only a game, but then again, not too softly. You are free to do as you wish. Let's begin—Are you ready?

Jack nods.

QUIZMASTER: "Six from Forty-five"—Forty-five men need work but only six can get work. Now are you prepared, Jack, to forego ten percent of your present pay?

JACK: Yes.
Jack slaps himself in the face. The audience applauds and laughs. Applause and laughter come from the television set.
QUIZMASTER: How about twenty percent?
JACK: Yes.
Jack slaps himself in the face. Audience laughs and applauds.
QUIZMASTER: Not so hard, old man
After all, it's only a game.
Now, how about thirty percent?
JACK: Yes.
Jack slaps himself in the face. Audience laughs.
QUIZMASTER: Forty percent?
JACK: Yes.
Jack slaps himself in the face and laughs. Audience laughs, too.
QUIZMASTER: Good work, Jack. Are you ready to drive three hours round trip to your place of employment?
JACK: Yes.
Jack slaps himself in the face and laughs. Audience laughter becomes louder and more sustained.
QUIZMASTER: How about four hours?
JACK: Yes.
Jack slaps himself in the face and laughs. Audience laughs long.
QUIZMASTER: Are you ready to perform any kind or work imaginable? Day or night? As far away from your home as possible? As bad as the work might be?
JACK: Yes. Yes. Yes.
Jack slaps himself in the face and laughs hysterically.
QUIZMASTER: Wonderful, Jack. That was the first round and you're still in the running.
Jack boxes his own ears with both hands and laughs. Audience howls with laughter.
QUIZMASTER: That's great!
The assistants Usche and Barbara bring in three dolls. Each doll wears a mask and coat.
QUIZMASTER: Now, old man, after your successful first round we have a particularly challenging second round. Pay attention. You were ready to do anything to get work. Without a doubt you wanted to be among the six from forty-five. But others

want it also. Let's take this guy, for example (*he points to the doll*). Let's say this is a colleague of yours, with whom you have worked, side-by-side, for ten years. Now he's jobless like you. Now he's competing for the same jobs you are—the very same one, in fact. Are you ready to knock your colleague from the field of competition? Then, go to it!

Jack attacks the doll. The doll falls to the floor with a comic flop. Audience applauds. Quizmaster points to another doll.

QUIZMASTER: And this, Jack, this guy is your own brother. If you still want to win, go to it, boy!

Jack attacks this doll as well. The doll falls to the floor with a comic flop. The audience applauds; Quizmaster points to the third doll.

QUIZMASTER: Now, Jack, now comes the most difficult challenge of all. Can you do it? Can you get a job? Not only your colleague, not only your brother—your own wife is eyeing your job. This doll is your own wife—If you want to win, Jack, go to it!

Jack raises his hand. The doll turns around. The mask is behind, in front one recognizes Diane's face. She looks at Jack. Silence. Jack lets his hand fall. The Quizmaster, the assistants, the whole quiz show set disappears in a cloud. Diane embraces Jack; Jack embraces Diane.

JACK: First, I'm going to take
              You to the Maldives
              For a long holiday.

DIANE: I've always told you
              You don't really have to go
              You just need to think about going.
              It's great if we just think about going—
              Together.

JACK: I can't imagine
              Going on like this.

DIANE: It will go on, Jack.
              Tomorrow, go to the Welfare Office
              I'll go to the bank
              And ask for an extension.
              Maybe you can go to the mill
              And apologize.
              And maybe I can get
              Odd jobs sewing.

JACK: Who am I to you, Diane?
DIANE: You're the dearest
You're the handsomest
You're the greatest.

They hold one another tightly.

JACK: Sometimes
The world is so easy.
You think that
All you have to do
Is push it a little bit
And it will bounce in front of you
Like a ball.

They hold one another tightly. Silence. A man in overalls enters the room. He watches the two, then laughs.

MAN: You don't see that every day.
A happy couple
The wife is pregnant
And the baby's room
Is already on its way.
Forward, folks!

The workers bring in a crib, still wrapped up.

JACK: Who's that?
MAN: (*laughs*) We are the baby's room
You ordered.
One crib—natural-wood finish—
Portable
One child's table
With activity board
One . . .

Jack shakes his head continuously. Suddenly, he jumps at the workers and would throw them out with all his might. Diane pulls him off the men.

DIANE: (*cries*) Please, Jack.
Let me have the baby's room.
Please, Jack—
I don't care—
They can take everything
The house
The television
Everything

					But not the baby
					Not the baby.
JACK:			(*cries out*) What baby, Diane?!
					What baby?
The workers, somewhat stunned, observe the scene. One worker begins to laugh uncontrollably.

Scene 8

The back room of a blue-jeans and digital-watch store. A Yugoslav fiddles with a video camera. A worker, quite drunk, sits on a pile of blue-jeans; he plays with his penis.

WORKER:			You foreign swine
					You absolute swine
					Man, pal
					I love you
					You have to believe me
					Life is crazy
					Crazy.
YUGOSLAV:		Yeah, life.
WORKER:			Should I explain to you
					Just what life is?
					Life is—pour away—
					Otherwise I can't get a hard-on
					Life is—backwards.
					When you're down, really down
					You're the greatest.
					Your old lady, the swine,
					Has left you—that's for sure.
					You stand alone in the flat
					And shout—you scream.
					Why not, no one's listening.
					It goes through the walls,
					Over the roofs and into
					The fucking sky.
					For a moment you're the whole
					Fucking world.
					You can cut apart the dolls
					And leave them lying around

	For as long as you want.
	For once you get things
	Your fucking way.
	You can tear up all her postcards
	All the fucking cities and sunsets
	And oceans—no one'll stop you.
	You glue your eyes shut and are
	Blind and powerful.
	No one can tell you to look at anything.
	That's the philosophy, pal.
YUGOSLAV:	Blind and powerful.

The Yugoslav positions his lighting.

WORKER:	This dick
	That hangs so limp and helpless
	Will rise again from defeat
	And harden into eternity.
YUGOSLAV:	Don't come until you get the sign.

Diane enters. She is heavily made up, wears a wig and sunglasses.

DIANE:	(*to Yugoslav*) Are you the one?
	A friend of mine sent me—
	For the money.
YUGOSLAV:	Sure, honey.
	Great, babe.
WORKER:	Cha-cha-cha
DIANE:	Is that the man I . . .
	I don't know much about movies.
WORKER:	Drop your panties
	Open your mouth—
	C'mon baby, light my fire
	I am lonely tonight.
YUGOSLAV:	He's a good guy
	A real good guy.
DIANE:	It's for the long holiday
	On the Maldives with my husband—
	And for the spending money
	To go with it.
WORKER:	Mr. Mojo risin'
	Mr. Mojo risin'.
DIANE:	I'm leaving.

WORKER: Lady, I am a graduate
Of the Technical College
I took special courses—
Mechanical drawing.
YUGOSLAV: A good guy
A really good guy.
DIANE: I've never done anything
Like this.
YUGOSLAV: It's easier
With music.
The Yugoslav presses the "play" button on the tape-recorder: one hears Yugoslav folk music.
YUGOSLAV: Please, honey
Take off your clothes.
Diane takes off her underwear, stuffing it into her pocketbook.
DIANE: How much do I get for this?
YUGOSLAV: First work,
Then pay.
DIANE: How much?
I've seen pictures of Yugoslavia
It's really quite nice down there
Cheap, too.
The worker crawls on all fours toward Diane.
WORKER: Beauty is only the flip side
Of shit.
She's made herself up
For someone else.
She laughed at his jokes
At the office party.
She showed me her shell
But it was only a hole
The waves of love and the ocean
I've been to school
But someone else's had the fun.
DIANE: Do I really have to moan?
YUGOSLAV: OK, we're rolling—
C'mon, honey, time to blow.
DIANE: Everything's happening
So quickly.

YUGOSLAV: Sure, fast—
Film's expensive.
Diane wipes the worker's penis with her handkerchief; then takes it in her mouth.
WORKER: Are you backwards, too?
Have you heard the droning
Of my endless nights?
The words I've exchanged
With the clothes you left behind?
Have you seen my tightened lips
When I burned your pictures in the ashtray
And held my hand over the flame?
I've filled the hole in that
Expensive marriage bed
With my angry fist.
Have they told you that I got drunk
In the parking lot at work?
With champagne?
The foreman looked through the windows
Of my car
Then the personnel manager
Then the company psychologist
Then company security
And I could have told them only one thing:
Your name.
Can you finally smell the stench
Of my burning heart?
YUGOSLAV: OK, now your turn.
Diane lies down, spreads her legs open wide; the worker puts his head between her legs.
WORKER: Dear mother,
At the edge of the playground
I looked for you.
In the coldness of the factory
I searched for your warmth.
At the Technical College
As a worker among rich kids
I listened for your voice.
You were always gone—
Yet I still lie with

	Heart and soul and tongue
	Before you.
YUGOSLAV:	OK, fuck now.

Worker climbs on top of Diane.

WORKER:	Shit, I can't.
DIANE:	I can't either.
YUGOSLAV:	Just think of something nice
	Back home in Cres
	The sun sets into the sea.
	To get in the boat and go out to watch it.
	To look down into the clear water
	And see the sun
	Just think of something nice.
DIANE:	The best was once
	When I worked in the kitchen.
WORKER:	The best is always
	In my dreams.

Diane caresses the worker. They make love. The Yugoslav approaches closely with the video camera so that he can focus in on the genitalia of both.

DIANE:	The cook always sent me
	Into the yard
	To wash off the lettuce.
	In the winter time
	My fingers got real red.
WORKER:	You will come back
	When I least expect you
	The empty bottles
	The empty hours
	The empty time
	The droning emptiness
	In an instant
	Everything will be gone.
DIANE:	One day the foreman
	Looked through the window
	From the bathroom
	And saw me—
	And the salad.
WORKER:	I'll make a drunken bow
	Propped up by your laughter
	So I won't fall.

DIANE:	He invited me in For a drink But I stayed At my post.
WORKER:	The muffled hours Day and night Will be heard again And there will be Endless conversation.
DIANE:	He came into the yard Took me by the hand And led me Past the cook Past the owner Past the guests To his table In the restaurant.
WORKER:	Things Won't be important anymore.
DIANE:	He ordered two glasses— Gin fizz— One for him And one for me. The owner's wife (It was the regular waitress's day off) Had to take our order.
YUGOSLAV:	OK, now come.
WORKER:	The touch
DIANE:	Never before
WORKER:	After such a long time
DIANE:	In my life.
WORKER:	It won't disappear into The Firmament of Poetry.
DIANE:	I drank the gin fizz.
WORKER:	Your cheeks
DIANE:	I drank it down in one gulp.
WORKER:	Beside my ear
DIANE:	Then another gulp
WORKER:	In my ear
DIANE:	And I didn't want it to stop.

WORKER: Beside your cheek.
The worker cries out. He falls on top of Diane. Both lie motionless on the floor. The Yugoslav picks up a violin and plays a tune.
YUGOSLAV: Let's record some moaning.
   First you, then the chick.
The worker and Diane get up and sit down on a pile of blue-jeans. The Yugoslav places a tape recorder in front of them.
DIANE: Loud?
YUGOSLAV: Normal.
WORKER: Ahhh. (*to Diane*)
   Can't hurt.
DIANE: Ahhh. (*to worker*)
   We own a house on Gasometer Street
   That is, we used to.
WORKER: Ahhh. (*to Diane*)
   My name is Fred Reiter
   I'm divorced and work as a
   Piece-work adjuster.
   That is, I used to.
DIANE: Ahhhh. (*to worker*)
   It wasn't as bad as I thought
   (*She introduces herself*)
   Freiberger, Diane Freiberger.
WORKER: Ahhh. May I buy you a drink?
   I'll behave myself.
DIANE: (*laughs*) Rum and Coke?
WORKER: (*smiles*) Ahhhh. . .
DIANE: That's what they give you
   On the Maldives—for free
   When you arrive there
   Compliments of the Travel Agency.
YUGOSLAV: Don't talk, just moan.
DIANE: Ahhh.
WORKER: Ahhhh.
DIANE: Ahhhhh.
WORKER: Ahhhhhh.
The pseudo-moaning quickly changes over into laughter.

Scene 9

A room in a "project" (public housing development). The only furnishing is furniture suited only for children. Jack sits in the crib—he is fairly drunk; Shakespeare lies on the floor, he, too, is drunk. Full and half-full beer bottles lie about. Jack watches a "cheap" porno film. He holds the remote control and stares vacantly at the television. Shakespeare opens a beer bottle and regards the bottle thoughtfully.

SHAKESPEARE: A full bottle
　　　　　　　Is the worst
　　　　　　　The fullness of the world—
　　　　　　　It just sits there so orderly
　　　　　　　Those neat little bottles
　　　　　　　In neat little rows
　　　　　　　Blindfolded by the labels.
　　　　　　　It still believes in itself
　　　　　　　And its usefulness at the supermarket.
　　　　　　　How wrong it is!

He drinks down the beer in one gulp—then regards the empty bottle with satisfaction.

SHAKESPEARE: An empty bottle
　　　　　　　Is the only truth
　　　　　　　It lies in the gutter somewhere
　　　　　　　And sees the world
　　　　　　　Like it is:
　　　　　　　The sunset shines off of it
　　　　　　　The dust from the street
　　　　　　　Covers it up
　　　　　　　The rain washes it off again
　　　　　　　It's serene in its cry
　　　　　　　An eye with no eyelid
　　　　　　　A stranger's steps are reflected in
　　　　　　　Its glass:
　　　　　　　It hears running and walking
　　　　　　　But that doesn't ruin its day.

He stands up with some effort, collecting four empties on his way.

SHAKESPEARE: And with the introduction of the
Aluminum can
The world has become just that much
Blinder.
He goes to Jack, placing the empties on the television set.
SHAKESPEARE: Jack.
These are my friends
The dead poets
They're all empties.
Shakespeare talks earnestly to Jack; Jack does not react.
SHAKESPEARE: *(points to the first bottle)*
Take this one, for instance, Jack.
My namesake, William Shakespeare
He was the greatest empty of them all.
He didn't lie in a field somewhere
Just looking at flowers
He saw it all.
He saw the bugs
He saw the women
He saw the good guys and the horses.
So still
So empty
So worthless.
He lay on the ground
So that all the voices of his age
Could echo in his stomach.
He poured it all out again—
The tender words of love—
The breathless tricks
And the loud cry of death.
Out over the heads of the bottlers
And damned them to an endless
Repetition of their sounds.
And when he'd had enough
He shattered himself so
Fundamentally
That no one really knows
Whether he ever existed.
Shakespeare points to the next bottle.

SHAKESPEARE: This is all that's left of
Heinrich Heine.
He was the palest of all the empties.
They tried to paint the German colors
On him
And he bore them for a long while
And bore them well.
Yet you always sensed a distance—
This Jew was never really
German
Because he just couldn't help himself
From throwing in a smart-ass last line.
They tossed this empty to Paris
Later on they simply gassed
People like him.
That was the final solution
For the empties problem.

Shakespeare points to the next bottle. Jack watches the porno film and does not react.

SHAKESPEARE: This one is Johann Wolfgang von Goethe.
The favorite empty of all Germans.
He drifted from the street into Government service.
He was never really empty to begin with
He ate too much bacon for that
I don't like him so much.

Shakespeare points to the next bottle. Jack doesn't react.

SHAKESPEARE: This is the unknown empty.
A young man before the last war
The great patriotic marches
Whistled in his ear
He wrote poems to their beat
He wrote in the trenches
He wrote in the field hospitals
He wrote and wrote
He believed victory was near—
A poetic one.
They brought him before a military court
They sent him to the munitions works
He made bullets

And wrote poems
Behind a mound of iron
And poetic victory was near
Then a pile of iron fell
Upon the poet's skull—
Crack and boom.
There were no more poems.
Just scattered words
And mad commentary.
The empty was shattered
It had to bear its broken shards
In its own head—
That's quite painful, too.

Shakespeare looks at Jack. Jack doesn't react. Silence.

SHAKESPEARE: I want to introduce you
To a few more friends, Jack.

Shakespeare goes to pick up a few more empty bottles.

JACK: Shut up, Shakespeare.

Jack stares at the television. He recognizes Diane in the film. He uses the remote control to move the film fast-forward, then backward. He switches to slow-motion. He repeats this action. Shakespeare comes over to him and watches the film, too. He, too, recognizes Diane. Jack is numb. Shakespeare looks at him. Silence. Shakespeare wants to comfort Jack, though he dares not.

SHAKESPEARE: Come over to the dead poets, Jack.
Come over to the gutter
A miracle happens there
When no one loves you anymore
When everyone passes you by
And every word is for someone else—
A miracle happens.
It's the day of resurrection
You see the world like you've never
Seen it before.
A painless view
You smile when you hear the screams
And you stay quiet
Amid the horror.

Silence. Diane enters the room. She is exhausted.

DIANE: You guys could at least
Pick up these empty bottles.
JACK: Diane?
C'mere.
DIANE: Yes, Jack?
JACK: Do you like me, Diane?
DIANE: I'm really tired, Jack.
I've been cleaning the whole day.
JACK: How much do you like me, Diane?
Do you like me as much
As I like you?

Jack rises slowly from the crib and staggers toward Diane.

JACK: Do you know
That I like you so much
That the moment I see you
I've gotta have you?
When you touch me
I feel it from head to toe.
It's not like that with other women, Diane.
Only with you.
Now, what about you?
Do you feel the same way when you see me?
Only with me?
Only with me?

Jack embraces Diane. He tries to pull her onto the floor.

DIANE: Stop it, Jack.
JACK: You want me to stop, Diane?
Why, Diane?
After all, I've always loved you.
When you sat next to me
On our way to see Iris
I thought even then—
It's really Diane I love.
And if she just says the word
I'll go off with her.
I'll be tender to her.
I'll take her clothes off—
Slowly . . .

Jack tried to disrobe Diane. She resists. Jack uses force to undress her.

DIANE: Are you crazy?
JACK: I'm crazy for you, Diane.
We've been sitting like this
For years, Diane
And I'm always thinking
When is she going to belong to me
When will she finally be just mine?
Diane begins to scream. Jack attempts to make love to her; a struggle ensues. Shakespeare takes a couple of empty beer bottles and places them on the floor next to the struggling husband and wife.
SHAKESPEARE: (*to the bottles*) Fellow poets—
What do I do now?
What do I do now?
Helpless, he laughs to himself.

Scene 10

In the blue-jeans and digital-watch store. It is noon ... The Yugoslav dozes behind the counter. The tape recorder plays Yugoslav folk music. Ringo enters the store; he is wearing a paramilitary uniform. He looks about carefully; he seems quite agitated. He sees the Yugoslav's violin and stares at it for quite awhile. He goes over to the Yugoslav, and shouts in his ear.

RINGO: Wake up, you fun-house freak!
Yugoslav almost falls from his chair; he jumps up, startled. Ringo laughs the wild laugh of a naughty child. The Yugoslav looks at Ringo suspiciously.
YUGOSLAV: What do you want?
Ringo becomes unsure. He keeps looking back at the door.
RINGO: How much is this watch?
YUGOSLAV: Not much.
RINGO: And the car radio?
YUGOSLAV: A lot.
RINGO: The postcard?
The Yugoslav becomes more suspicious.
YUGOSLAV: What do you want?
RINGO: No. Why don't you tell me
How much this postcard costs?

YUGOSLAV: You, go away
From my store.
RINGO: Why don't you go away?
Jack, the Italian and Shakespeare enter the store. Shakespeare is holding a beer stein, filled to the brim; Jack glares at the Yugoslav.
ITALIAN: (*to the Yugoslav*)
Ah, my friend from the competition.
Makes cheap porno
Uses local models
And ruins my business.
The Italian goes over to the video shelf and takes out a cassette. He pulls the video band out of the cassette.
ITALIAN: Bad films
No plot
No imagination
Just pure sex.
Yugoslav pushes the Italian away.
ITALIAN: And violence.
YUGOSLAV: You, leave that alone.
RINGO: You leave our women alone
Just leave our women alone
You'd better leave our women alone.
Schmelzer and Ursus enter the store. Ursus pulls a welding cart into the store. Schmelzer holds a steel pipe and pipe pliers. Ringo and the Italian greet Schmelzer and Ursus as they enter. The Yugoslav becomes increasingly nervous.
YUGOSLAV: I don't need that in the shop
Get it out!
SCHMELZER: We need it for a little
Demonstration, my friend.
We were quite impressed
When you used the wife
Of a buddy of ours
For one of your films.
We thought that maybe
We might be able to
Impress you a little, too.
JACK: (*to the Yugoslav*) Where did she do it?
Diane, I mean
Did she do it here?

SCHMELZER: (*to Jack*) Calm down, son.
Calm down.
(*to Yugoslav*)
Watch it, my friend.
You've brought us a step closer
To Hollywood.
Now we'll bring you a step closer
To the Steel Mill.
I am holding in my hand
A simple steel pipe.
Approximately three feet in length
Two inches in diameter
And one and a half inches thick.
One end is open
The other closed.
This is a special type of pliers
We use them to hold red-hot steel.
Ringo, lock the door.

Schmelzer tosses the pliers to the Italian. Ringo goes to the door, locks it. The Yugoslav tries to flee through a side room; Ursus grabs him.

SCHMELZER: What's the rush, pal?
The show is just starting.
Now here you see a complete
Welding apparatus:
Consisting of the cart
Two tanks
Hoses, welding iron
And the so-called torch
Or blow-torch.
We open the vent on the gas tank
Light the gas
At the end of the torch.

Schmelzer ignites the gas with a match. The flame burns. He turns the dial slowly open on the oxygen tank. The flame becomes smaller, more intense.

SCHMELZER: The real welding flame
Begins when you turn on
The oxygen.
Now we come to the climax of our show—
The heating up of the steel.

The Italian pulls down the Yugoslav's pants and places the pipe over his penis. He holds the pipe in place with the pliers. Schmelzer holds the welding flame at the closed end of the pipe. The Yugoslav watches in numbed silence. Ursus holds him in his powerful clutches. The end of the pipe slowly begins to heat up. The Yugoslav groans.

JACK: How did she do it—
Diane, I mean.
Why don't you moan
Like she did.
C'mon, moan.

Shakespeare watches the scene. His whole body shakes.

SHAKESPEARE: Fire consumes friend and foe
She hears no pleas for help
You can't appeal to her sense
Of Justice.
Turn if off, Schmelzer.

Schmelzer continues his work.

SHAKESPEARE: Turn it off, Schmelzer!

SCHMELZER: Shakespeare
Why don't you come over here
Take the torch.

SHAKESPEARE: No, thanks.
I'm shaking too much
I'd burn my hands.
And my face would catch on fire
My thoughts
My words
Would disappear in the heat.
Turn off the flame
When you guys do nothing
I'll drink
I'm a lonely
Fireplug anyway.

He drinks a beer in one gulp.

SCHMELZER: Ringo, show him
What we do to friends
Who don't go along.

Ringo goes toward Shakespeare. Shakespeare presses close to the wall.

RINGO: Whose side are you on?
SHAKESPEARE: That's the question
Wherever I stood
It was never enough.
Hardly had I taken my place
In the rank and file
Sang their songs
When I got a crazy thought.
I've already bailed out—
I'm sorry, Ringo
I suffer from Philosophical cold feet.
RINGO: Bullshitter.

Ringo grabs Shakespeare by the neck and drags him to the welder. Schmelzer forces the blowtorch into his hand. Shakespeare shakes—the blowtorch, too.

SCHMELZER: Now you're standing here

The Yugoslav groans.

SHAKESPEARE: Couldn't you turn down
The flame
Just a bit?
SCHMELZER: Nope.
The flame isn't even hot yet—
Turn it up.

Shakespeare looks to Jack; Jack looks back at Shakespeare.

SHAKESPEARE: The torch
Stays amazingly cool
Maybe violence and force
Is nothing more than a dial
That innocently turns
And bears another's burdens, eh?

He turns the oxygen further open. The flame intensifies. The Yugoslav groans loudly. Shakespeare closes his eyes.

SHAKESPEARE: I can feel only
The cool blow-torch.
SCHMELZER: Keep going.

He turns the dial open. The Yugoslav begins to scream in pain. Shakespeare opens his eyes. The workers look at him. They smile and nod.

SHAKESPEARE: I wanted to give you guys

Everything.
I've been piling books up for forty years
You guys have avoided those piles
The greatest mountains on earth
And I never knew
How easy it was to get you to smile.

The Yugoslav screams.

SHAKESPEARE: What can you do
When all this smiling
Drowns out that
Horrible noise?

Ursus lets one hand free from the Yugoslav and takes his turn at the pipe.

URSUS: What's he screaming about
This thing isn't even hot
Yet.

The Yugoslav screams.

JACK: Diane
Diane screamed
Didn't she
How did she scream—
I wanna hear
I wanna hear.

Jack's screaming turns to sobbing. Shakespeare drops the blowtorch, runs to the refrigerator, takes out a bottle of schnapps and drinks. The Yugoslav begins to sing a Serbo-Croatian song. Ringo laughs and makes odd gestures. Schmelzer puts on protective glasses, takes the blow-torch and turns the oxygen dial completely open. The flame reaches its most intense heat. Then, a transformation: the light coming from the welding flame and its sparks illuminates the entire stage.

JACK: Oh, Diane
I have found
The virgin beaches
Of your body

YUGOSLAV: When I was fifteen
I took a boat and
Rowed so long that
I couldn't see my village anymore.

JACK: With a wandering tongue
I rowed through the meadows
Of your moist curls.
YUGOSLAV: When I was twenty
I got on a train
And went so far that
I couldn't understand the
Language anymore
JACK: I took my yearning lips
Through the small folds
Of your tender breasts.
YUGOSLAV: By the time I was thirty
I had been everywhere
I could imitate the local dialect
Even their gestures—perfectly.
But when I thought
I had become one of them—
They drove me out.
JACK: Your shoulders
Are the cradles
Which invite me back
With every drowsy love.
YUGOSLAV: Today I'd like to build a ship
And sail down the river
To the sea.
JACK: How can I ever manage
To leave these places
These valleys, fields and streams
These pasts and presents
Turn my back on them
And leave?
YUGOSLAV: I'd like to show up
In my village
On a Sunday morning
When the square is empty
And all you hear is the voices
Of men and women in church.

The Yugoslav falls to the floor, sobbing. Jack kneels on the floor, also sobbing. Schmelzer turns off the welding apparatus. End of transformation. Normal stage lighting. An awkward

silence. One hears only the sobs of Jack and the Yugoslav. Shakespeare crawls on all fours to Jack.
SHAKESPEARE: Can I cry with you, Jack?
Jack looks up briefly.
JACK: Go away.
Shakespeare crawls to the Yugoslav.
SHAKESPEARE: How 'bout with you, pal?
Can I cry with you?
The Yugoslav pushes Shakespeare away. Shakespeare crawls to the middle of the room. He looks at the Italian, Schmelzer and Ringo. One after the other.
SHAKESPEARE: And you guys?
Can I laugh with you?
The three look away, embarrassed.
SHAKESPEARE: No?
Well, then I'll laugh by myself.
Shakespeare tries to laugh. One sees only a grimace—there is no sound.

Scene 11

The living room of the Minister for Commerce and Labor, somewhere in the capital city. The Minister sits in front of a television, watching a video tape of his latest speeches—without sound. He watches his image. Whenever a gesture or facial expression does not please him, he stops the picture to practice and refine the gesture or expression. After this, he continues the tape. The Minister's wife and a fat American female singer sit at the coffee table, drinking coffee.

AMERICAN: My last time-travel experience was awful. It took me to Connecticut in 1690. I was a young, beautiful girl and lived in a simple cabin at the edge of the woods. Nearby there was a village—English who had come to America to begin a new life. They were horribly puritanical—always wore dark clothes and even on Sunday no one was allowed any fun. My parents were dead and my only friends were the Indians. They loved me because I loved nature just as much as they did. The English saw in nature only an enemy who had to be conquered. One day an Englishman rode by just when I was taking a bath. I was naked, of course. He took one look at me and I felt right away that he loved me and hated me at the same time. He spread nasty stories about me in the village—that I was crazy and that I was a dangerous person. Then I fell in love with an Indian and had a child by him. The women in the village thought the father was one of their husbands; and they began to hate me, too. They couldn't see that the child looked Indian, they were that blind in their hatred. Then, the man who had seen me in the bath happened to kill another man during a hunt. The rumor started up that I had put a curse on the man and so they brought me to trial. I was condemned to death. They tied me to the ground and piled stones on me—they literally crushed me to death. God, I looked like a pancake.

MINISTER: Elsa! Pardon me, please.

The Minister's wife goes to her husband.

MINISTER: Who is this nut?

WIFE: She's an American singer. I met her at the spa. She goes on time travels.

MINISTER: She does what?

WIFE: She puts people in a trance and takes them back to a former life. She's been on television.

MINISTER: What? Give me a break.

WIFE: Well, didn't you say you wanted to be exposed to all the newest trends?

MINISTER: Elsa, dear, could you be so kind and tell that woman to get her fat ass into the next room. I'm practicing.

WIFE: Well, you don't have to put it like that.

The doorbell rings.

MINISTER: Of course, I have to put it like that. I have a mistress and I can say anything I want in my house: Shit, shit shit shit shit! Dear, the doorbell.

The Minister's wife goes into the hallway. The Minister concentrates on his image on the television screen. The American singer sings an aria from the opera, "La Traviata."

AMERICAN: I just love this opera, don't you, Mr. Minister?

MINISTER: I love my country, I love my party, I love my family and I love the opera; so fuck off, fatso.

AMERICAN: Excuse me?

MINISTER: Just kidding.

The Minister's wife returns to the room, accompanied by Jack. Jack is dressed in a suit and tie. Although he is well-groomed, he appears somewhat pitiful. He seems to be a broken man. The Minister looks at him.

MINISTER: Is this the next exhibit for your little freak show? What's he doing here?

WIFE: (*laughs*) A worker from the depressed area.
He says he needs a job.

Minister looks at his wife; looks at Jack, looks at the American, looks back at his wife.

MINISTER: Who loves me around here anymore?
Has it ever entered anyone's mind
That I'm human, too?
I have needs, too, you know.
When I leave this house in the morning
Even the chauffeur asks me
Whether I can help his nephew get
Government-subsidized housing.
When I walk onto the floor of Parliament
The porter asks me to see if I can fix it with
The bank to give him a loan.
At the office my secretary asks me
To get her friend a job.
The "loyal opposition" demands my resignation
Reporters sniff around into my past
And everybody wants jobs.
Shit. Shit. Shit. Shit.
D'you know what I'd like to do?
I don't want to live anymore—Fuck it, over.
I don't want to live anymore.

WIFE: Then go ahead and kill yourself.
If you've got the time for it in your
Busy schedule, that is.

MINISTER: Thank you.

The American singer examines Jack from all sides. Jack is completely disturbed by this.

AMERICAN: Yes, he is a medium
I can see his aura.
What's your name, darling?

JACK: (*toward the Minister*)
My name is Jack Freiberger
I used to be a steelworker.
Mr. Minister, you said on television
That the people were your main concern.
Well, I'm one of the people.

He begins to cry.

JACK: And so I thought
I'll go to the Minister
And ask about a job.
You see, I've been charged with
Assault and battery
And the baby's room is already
Set up in our place.

MINISTER: I don't get it.

The American singer takes Jack by the hand and leads him to a chair.

AMERICAN: Come here, darling, calm down
Relax.

She sits him down softly in the chair.

AMERICAN: We'll take a trip back in time, OK?
Close your eyes and breathe calmly, deeply.
I will help you.
Relax your body, relax completely:
The present is leaving you behind
Your breathing is calm and deep
Suddenly, in front of your inner eye . . .

JACK: Diane.
Diane is out of work, too.
The appliance factory moved to Spain.
I was Schmelzer's first assistant
They fired me because of the business
In the company canteen.
They fired Ringo, too.
But the mortgage payments kept coming.

AMERICAN: You have to move into yourself, baby—
Not outward—inward.

JACK: But the baby's room
Was already on order—
Then Diane went to the Yugoslav

| | And made a movie.
| | We only wanted to scare the guy
| | And now they've charged me
| | With assault and battery.
| MINISTER: | A social minidrama.
| | A few unpaid bills, a little assault and battery.
| | I've heard it a hundred times before.
| | C'mon lady, take me back in time—
| | I want to show you what drama is.

The Minister pushes Jack from the chair and sits down there himself.

MINISTER: OK, let's go, lady, turn on your magic.

The American singer claps her hands excitedly.

AMERICAN: Place your hands on your knee
            Close your eyes.
            Breathe deeply and calmly.
            Deeply and calmly. Deeply and calmly.
            Don't think of the present—
            Just set your mind on the past.
            Your inner eye will open up . . .
MINISTER: I see
            I see the turn of the century—
            But not the way they show it in books
            Or art exhibits. No, I see the time in all
            Its sociological horror.
            I see the steel mill, I see the blast furnace—
            But not the modern kind where everything is done
            By computer. I see a giant pit where the steel
            Brews—I see the heavy chains hanging from the ceiling
            I see the dust and the darkness.
            I see the tortured faces of the steelworkers.
            And, in the middle of this conglomeration of steel,
            Dust, sweat and darkness I see myself—
            A simple working man.
            The women drag the buckets of slag
            The children squeal at their feet.
JACK: They have a day-care center at the mill now.
AMERICAN: Shut up, baby.
            He's inside, he's inside now.

MINISTER: What an inferno.
Suddenly a chain breaks loose from its mooring
We run and scream, but the chain starts to fall
It buries a man next to me
With our collective might we pull the chain
From his body—he's still breathing
What do we do?
JACK: Get the company doctor!
The American gestures for Jack to be quiet.
MINISTER: There is no company doctor for the lowest of the low.
A vague anger, an inner rage grabs hold of me.
I take a board, the nearest thing to me.
We lay his crushed body on the board
We carry it into the Main Hall—he's still alive.
We carry him across the yard
And into the front yard of the mill owner.
We go up to the house, the smells of wealth encircle us.
Our faces are dark—We knock on the door.
No one opens from the other side
We beat the door in—
We hear the cries of the owner's wife fleeing out the door.
The mill owner isn't at home—he's out hunting.
We lay our dying friend down in the finest silks.
We feel the bitterness and tears
He dies.
And then again the anger, the swelling up of wrath inside.
I rip a red curtain from the window, tie it onto a stick
And run around waving it, even though I'm not the type
You'd expect to do something like that.
I run into the mill yard, yelling,
"Our brother is dead! The Capitalist mugs
Are to blame again! The satanic thugs who're killing mankind."
And from every part of the factory the workers stream out

They join me and we move from the factory yard,
   past the
Front gate into the street.
Then, suddenly in front of us—mounted police!
The paid assassins of the rich and famous!
Then, silence. A long silence.
The bullies wade through us. Again silence.
And again the same anger inside of me.
I hold the flag high, I march I cry, "Brothers!
On to freedom! Onto our place in the sun!"
Then, a shot rings out. I'm hit.
Slowly, an eternity, it seems, the flag falls to
   earth.
My breath stops, my eye closes
I'm dead.

He opens his eyes. The American applauds enthusiastically. The Minister jumps up.

MINISTER: Children, I haven't felt so good
For a long time.

He looks at Jack.

MINISTER: Don't look so glum, my friend.
What can I do for you?
I'm ready to perform any act of graft.
You need work, don't you?
And work you'll get
Work you'll get.

The Minister hooks his arm onto Jack's and goes with him about the room.

MINISTER: Brothers, we demand our place in the sun!
On to freedom!
On to a new age!

Scene 12

The Personnel Office of the Steel Mill. The new Personnel Manager sits behind his desk. Jack sits in front of the desk. The Manager examines Jack. Silence. The Personnel Manager folds a piece of paper into an airplane and lets it float through the room. Jack stands up; he picks up the paper airplane and places it back on the Manager's desk. The Manager looks at him suspiciously.

MANAGER: Why did you pick that up? What are you trying to prove by that? Are you trying to brown-nose me? Do you want to bribe me? Turn this thing to your own advantage? Am I supposed to turn a blind eye to your mistakes just because you're a favorite of mine? Suspicious, very suspicious. *The Personnel Manager regards Jack with deep mistrust. Jack does not understand what this is all about. Silence. Suddenly, the Personnel Manager changes his expression, laughs and shakes Jack's hand with both hands.*

MANAGER: Congratulations—you're the new steward. God knows how you fixed it so that the Minister himself intervened for you. But you did it. The criminal charge against you was dropped; you've gotten a place in the new housing development and you've gotten a new promotion. Whattaya have to say for yourself now?

JACK: Whattaya mean "Steward"?
I'm a steelworker
I wanna go back to the
Blast furnace.

MANAGER: That's very interesting—here's a guy who doesn't want to go up, he wants to go down. What's the point of this maneuver—Do you want to make us in the office look bad? What are we supposed to tell the Minister in two weeks when he phones about you and we tell him we've given you some shitty job back in the mill? Are you trying to get us blacklisted because we didn't do exactly like he asked us to do? Very clever, very clever.

JACK: No, but...

MANAGER: But what?

Jack is silent.

MANAGER: OK, fine. You're the new steward. Here's the list of current slackers. Go into the mill and simply see how your old pals are working.

JACK: But that's not real work—
Watching my old buddies work.

MANAGER: That's the most difficult work there is—our whole existence depends on you. There are those who work and those who watch the workers work. Those who don't fill their quota we put on the list. Whoever doesn't show up or takes too many cigarette breaks or who whines too much we put on the list. You see, we need names. Names. Names. Lists filled with names. Everyday the politicians announce on television that another thousand or two thousand workers have been laid off. We've got to be ready, the lists have to be ready, doncha see?

JACK: Sure.

MANAGER: Now what do you do to the guy who works too much, who volunteers for overtime?

JACK: Don't put him on the list.

MANAGER: Are you so sure? What's that guy trying to prove with all his hustle? Isn't he trying to make it more difficult for us to lay off people? Isn't he trying to see to it that we just have to make more steel that we can't sell anyway? Isn't he trying to drive us into a bigger crisis than the one we already have? He's a suspicious character—put him on the list. Now, do you understand the system?

JACK: I'm not sure.

MANAGER: What do you think of a guy who sits on the toilet for too long?

JACK: Maybe he has diarrhea.

MANAGER: Maybe. As you know we don't have television cameras in the stalls. Maybe a guy writes a letter to the editor of a Communist paper, maybe he's noticed that the factory toilets have newspapers for the toilets while in the office toilets they have real smooth toilet paper. You can't trust a man like that. He's suspicious—put him on the list. Next case. Let's say an employee hurts himself—not seriously—but let's say he cut himself on the arm. What do you do?

JACK: I'd take him
To the company doctor.

MANAGER: Sure, you take him to the company doctor. But what can you expect of a guy who abuses our medical facilities the way he does. Doesn't he know that this system barely pays for itself anyway? Does he want to exploit our already shaky welfare system? Do you understand what this is all about? Everyone and everything is suspicious. Look around my office—what do you see?

Jack looks about.

JACK: Nothing.

MANAGER: And this picture?

JACK: A tree.
MANAGER: Sure, a tree. A tree in full bloom. Seems a pretty common sight, doesn't it?
JACK: Yes, pretty common.
MANAGER: Well, why does the tree have leaves on it? What does the artist have in mind? Does he want to tell us that this is one of the last trees around with leaves on it? Does he want to say that all the other trees are dead or dying? Does he want to indict our whole socio-industrial complex? Does he think all this activity, our economical miracle, has been a giant mistake? Put him on the list. Are you married?
JACK: Yes.
MANAGER: Me, too.

He shows Jack a photograph.

MANAGER: What do you think of my wife?
JACK: She plays piano?
MANAGER: Yes, in fact, she does play the piano. When I come home at night, she's always playing the piano. What does she mean by that? That I'm some uncultured boob who only has time for business and career and numbers, while she can appreciate the finer things like culture? We haven't slept together for years, does she mean to indicate my sexual dysfunction by fucking around on the piano? Does she have a lover she sees during the day? A student, maybe? Who can fit her into his schedule? What does she talk about with him? Music? Don't make me laugh. I know all about these types of relationships. He falls on top of her, she jumps on top of him. They fuck like dogs. And when she sits there sweetly playing piano—he's getting back his sexual powers instead of studying. The guy probably gets a scholarship—that's how it works these days. What do you think of my wife now? And what about me? What do you think of me? Aren't you suspicious about me, too?
JACK: I don't know.
MANAGER: Think back. Up until a short while ago a woman sat behind this desk. What happened to her? Why did I get the job? Did you know that our late-lamented Personnel Manager only liked women. Maybe I tipped off someone in the head office—anonymously, of course—about her Lesbian tendencies? Or maybe she left because she couldn't fill the layoff

quotas. Dear Sir, it is time you took notice—Man is hell. He can only survive when he pushes another out of the way. You would like to get me out of the way, too—wouldn't you?
The Manager glares penetratingly at Jack.
MANAGER: But I will beat you to it. I will get you out of the way.
He pulls a pistol from his jacket and takes aim at Jack. Jack holds his hands in front of his face. The Manager pulls the trigger. A flame comes from the barrel of the gun—the pistol is a cigarette lighter.
MANAGER: Cigarette?
Manager lets loose a hearty belly laugh . . .

Scene 13

An apartment in the "projects." Evening. Everything is neat and orderly. A cold cut platter lies on the table. Jack spreads mustard on his sandwich. Diane comes out of the kitchen. She is obviously pregnant. She is setting the table.

JACK: Diane
Can you remember
What I said a long time ago?
You know, how someone who's slaved
At the mill all these years can't just be
Turned out like that from his job.
I'll be back, I said
I'll show everyone, I said
Did I say it
Or didn't I say it?
DIANE: What're you doing, Jack?
JACK: When the Minister called me "Jack"
I knew things were looking up
(loudly)
And things are looking up!
Are you happy now, Diane?
Is it just like you thought
It would be?

DIANE: I thought
That we would put the mustard alongside
Who ever wants mustard
Can help himself.
JACK: I mean life, Diane.
DIANE: What about life, Jack?
JACK: Are you happy?
DIANE: Sure.
Jack grabs Diane by the back of her head.
JACK: I want to know if you're really happy, Diane.
You know, sometimes I'd like to be able
To see inside—to see
What your dreams look like—
Do you still dream of long walks in the woods
Of taking long ocean cruises?
DIANE: I don't have dreams anymore, Jack.
Jack releases her.
JACK: Nowadays you can't afford dreams.
Is the beer cold enough, Diane. . ?
DIANE: Yes, Jack.
JACK: Schmelzer's gotta have his ice-cold
Ever since I've been a steward
He hasn't said a word to me.
But that's just temporary—
It'll change
It'll change
I know the old bastard
When I came to the mill
Ten years ago
It was the same thing—
He didn't say a word to me.
Then I became his best pal
His son, almost
He even said so once.
DIANE: Where are your friends, Jack?
They shoulda been here long ago.
JACK: Don't get excited, Diane,
They'll be here, you'll see
They'll be here.
I put the invitations in their lockers

It said "Food and Drink"
And in parentheses I put
All you want

Jack laughs—Diane looks at him.

DIANE: They're not going to show up, Jack.
JACK: You worry about the food—
I'll worry about the rest.

Diane goes to the kitchen. Jack watches the clock. He takes a beer and drinks. Diane brings soup into the room and places the bowl on the table. Silence.

DIANE: What's wrong now, Jack?
Silence.
JACK: Why don't you put the soup back on the stove
Otherwise, it'll get cold.

Diane takes the soup-bowl back into the kitchen. The doorbell rings. Jack breathes a sigh of relief, he smiles. Diane brings the soup-bowl back onto the table.

JACK: Quick, light the candles.

Diane lights the candles; Jack goes to the door, opens it, Shakespeare is standing on the other side: drunk. He collects himself somewhat, however. He has a bouquet of flowers in his hand. He has dressed himself up—unfortunately he still appears rather disorderly and unkempt.

JACK: Shakespeare—You?
Where are the others?
SHAKESPEARE: What others?
JACK: Schmelzer, Ringo
The Italian, Ursus—
Where are they?
SHAKESPEARE: Oh, those others.
They'll be here later.
JACK: Whatta ya mean "later"?
SHAKESPEARE: I mean, they'll be here soon.
JACK: Shakespeare, old pal
C'mon in.
Diane, look who's here—
Our old friend, Shakespeare.

Shakespeare enters the room slowly.

SHAKESPEARE: *(to Diane)* Hello.
Nice place here
Very nice.

Shakespeare gives Diane the flowers.
DIANE: Thank you.
Shakespeare bows comically.
JACK: That wasn't really necessary—
C'mere, old pal
Sit down—
Diane, our guest is hungry.
Diane serves up soup to Shakespeare. Jack offers him a sandwich.
JACK: Dig in, Shakespeare, dig in.
There's plenty more
Now tell us
How're you doing?
I'm doin' fine—you can see that.
It's no house in the suburbs
But still . . .
The apartment has a bedroom
A living room, a children's room
And the rest . . .
You know, hallway, closets and stuff like that.
Utilities are low—
Real low.
Shakespeare chews his sandwich, but finds it difficult to swallow.
JACK: Are you thirsty, Shakespeare?
Why didn't you say so?
Diane, our guest is thirsty!
A beer for Mr. Shakespeare.
Diane places a beer before Shakespeare; Jack looks at the bottle.
JACK: Not this cheap stuff, Diane—
Get the good beer.
Diane takes the bottle back into the kitchen; she shakes her head as she goes.
JACK: Right, Shakespeare?
Do we celebrate our resurrection
That calls for a special
Kind of beer.
Diane gestures to Jack.
DIANE: Jack, could I see you for a minute, please?
Jack gets up.

JACK: (*to Shakespeare*)
When the boss calls
You don't ask questions.

Jack goes over to Diane. The two converse in low tones.

DIANE: What do you mean "special" beer, Jack?
We've only got one kind!!

JACK: But I told you only the best
For my friends!

DIANE: Jack, your friends
Aren't going to show up.

JACK: You'll see—
They'll show up.

Shakespeare stands up and goes about the apartment, checking it out. Jack and Diane do not notice him as they talk.

DIANE: I don't know.
What it's like for you
At the mill, Jack.
You never tell me anything,
But since you've been named steward
Nobody in our building will talk with me.
I used to think
That if I had a child
That if we made enough money
That if I had you—
Then I didn't need anybody else.
But now I have all that
I *do* need people.
I need them to ask me
How I'm feeling
How my baby is
Or just how we like our new place.
It's so quiet out there.
Since there've been so many layoffs
I have the feeling
No one talks to anyone else.
No, they're not going to show up tonight, Jack.

JACK: They have to!
I'll tell them why
I became a steward—
Not for me, Diane,

　　　　　　　Not for me
　　　　　　　But for the baby,
　　　　　　　That's the truth.
　　　　　　　You can't have an expectant mother
　　　　　　　Living in mill housing—
　　　　　　　They'll understand that.
　　　　　　　Then I'll tell them
　　　　　　　Do they really think that
　　　　　　　I'd put them on the list?
　　　　　　　I put everyone else on the list,
　　　　　　　But not them!
　　　　　　　Schmelzer will put his arm around me and say,
　　　　　　　"Son, I understand.
　　　　　　　I was wrong about you."
　　　　　　　And that'll be it.
　　Diane looks at Jack. An uneasy silence follows. Then, the doorbell.
JACK:　　　　They really are going to show!
　　Jack runs to the door, opens it: Shakespeare, again, he stumbles into the apartment; embraces Jack.
SHAKESPEARE: Come to me, my son
　　　　　　　I'm Schmelzer, the bare-headed,
　　　　　　　The defiant one!
JACK:　　　　(*screams*) Stop it, Shakespeare!
　　Jack pushes Shakespeare away.
SHAKESPEARE: I'm Schmelzer, the bare-headed
　　　　　　　The defiant one!
　　　　　　　My head is free and unencumbered
　　　　　　　And unencumbered it'll stay.
　　　　　　　I need daylight between me and danger.
　　　　　　　The shit comes from above
　　　　　　　My head can smell it
　　　　　　　And I leap out of the way
　　　　　　　In the nick of time.
　　Shakespeare hops around the apartment—he tries to make Jack laugh.
JACK:　　　　Please, Shakespeare
　　　　　　　Stop it.
SHAKESPEARE: I'm Schmelzer
　　　　　　　Here inside this hell

	Beside this furnace
	Beside my sons
	I don't smell the shit here.
JACK:	You're not Schmelzer
	You're Shakespeare.
SHAKESPEARE:	Where are my sons?
	They've taken them from me
	One by one.
	I am the branch
	They can prune and burn.
	Put me on the list, Jack.
	I'll volunteer—I'll jump right in
	I've been burned out for a long time.
JACK:	No. No.
SHAKESPEARE:	No?
	I'm always the one
	Left over.
	I'm the Lord of this Hell
	I'm immortal.

Jack cries out. Suddenly he jumps at Shakespeare, grabs his neck and tries to strangle him.

JACK:	Schmelzer! Schmelzer!
SHAKESPEARE:	(*struggling to breathe*)
	I'm not Schmelzer!
	I'm Shakespeare!
JACK:	Schmelzer!
	You're not immortal
	They told me to put you on the list
	And when you're gone
	The heart is out
	The furnace goes
	And the mill dies.
SHAKESPEARE:	(*struggling to breath*)
	Jack, Jack . . .

Jack releases Shakespeare; Shakespeare falls to the ground and struggles to catch his breath. Diane helps him.

JACK:	Schmelzer—How could you think
	That I'd put you on the list?
	No, Schmelzer, I won't do that.
	But you know what I will do?
	I'll put myself on the list—
	That's what I'll do.

Scene 14

Darkened stage. Jack stands on the stage and looks into the audience. He wears the uniform of a mill steward and holds the list of layoffs. He writes his own name on the list. He places the list on the stage floor—the list remains there until the end of the play. Jack turns around; he stands with his back to the audience. The stage becomes gradually brighter. A several-meter-high pear-shaped pot is seen—an idealized blast furnace. A winding staircase leads to the top. Above is a bridge. The dark red reflection of the boiling steel illuminates the stage. All characters of the play stand on the bridge above. Beside the "furnace" stand the Quizmaster and his two assistants, Schmelzer, Ringo, the Steward, and Minister and his wife, the first Personnel Manager, the worker from the porno film, the American singer and Ursus. The Italian, the Yugoslav, the waitress, Shakespeare and Diane stand on the winding stairway. The second Personnel Manager stands on the bridge. Jack goes from one to another, saying good-bye. The Quizmaster clasps him by the hand and pats him on the shoulder.

QUIZMASTER: You were really good. You could've almost made it.
Jack smiles and moves on. He stops in front of Schmelzer. Schmelzer turns his face away from Jack.
JACK: Why didn't you show up, Schmelzer?
When I was a kid
And my father hung himself
From the window ledge
I thought to myself
Now I know that you can die
But come on down again, please
He didn't come down from the window ledge.
Why didn't you show up?
Silence.
JACK: Why did you leave me?
Jack smiles and moves on. He stands in front of Ringo.
JACK: Ringo.
Can you play a good-bye song?

RINGO: I'm sorry, Jack.
After I was laid off
I smashed the clarinet into
A thousand pieces.
JACK: Play anyway. . .
Ringo looks insecurely to Schmelzer. He presses his hands to his mouth and plays a short tune. It's a pleasant tune.
JACK: Thanks.
Jack smiles and moves on. He stands before the former Steward.
STEWARD: Look, Jack.
I'll dance again for you.
Steward does a short dance in front of Jack.
STEWARD: Since I've quit being a steward
I dance in restaurants
And at weddings.
Sometimes they laugh at me.
Sometimes they invite me to dinner
And sometimes I even get money.
Jack smiles and moves on. He stands before the Minister and his wife. The Minister shakes his hands—both of them.
MINISTER: I hear you're leaving the mill? Too bad. Somehow I liked you.
Jack smiles and moves on. He moves past the first Personnel Manager. He stops before the worker from the porno film.
JACK: I don't know you.
WORKER: I'm the one who slept with your wife.
Jack smiles and moves on. He moves on to the American singer. He stands before Ursus. Jack smiles. He caresses Ursus's face.
JACK: Ursus, old pal.
URSUS: You know, I used to like you.
But since you've been a Steward
I'm not allowed
To like you anymore.
Jack smiles and moves on. The Italian stands before him.
JACK: What do you have to tell me?
ITALIAN: (*smiles an embarrassed smile*)
Ciao, Jack.

Jack smiles and moves on. By now he has reached the bottom of the stairs. He stops in front of the Yugoslav.
JACK: I really hated you.
I'd like to apologize
For that now.
YUGOSLAV: My bags are already packed.
I have nothing more to
Do with you people.
Jack smiles and moves on. The waitress stands before him.
WAITRESS: Would you like a farewell beer, Jack?
It's on the house.
Jack smiles and kisses the waitress. He moves on. He stands before Shakespeare. Shakespeare stares at him; Jack smiles.
JACK: Shakespeare
Why are you looking at me like that?
I'd like to say good-bye to you
Can we shake hands?
Shakespeare looks numbly at Jack; Jack embraces him. Shakespeare doesn't move. Jack smiles and moves on. He comes to Diane. He places his hand on her stomach and tries to smile.
DIANE: Where are you going, Jack?
Silence. Diane clings to Jack.
DIANE: Take me with you, Jack
Take me with you.
PERSONNEL MANAGER: (*from above*) Mr. Freiberger?
Shouldn't we finish up with the
Formalities?
JACK: (*to Diane*)
Once in life I'd like to be like you, Diane.
I'd like to close me eyes and dream.
I'd like to dream about
All those possibilities
You have in life.
Jack moves away from Diane and climbs the winding stairs. Shakespeare follows him a few steps behind. Jack reaches the bridge. He stands next to the Personnel Manager. Jack removes his Steward's coat and gives it to the Personnel Manager.
MANAGER: Your file: pay stubs, work record, tax receipts. Would you like to say something before you go? Do you have a last request? A cigarette, perhaps?

The Personnel Manager offers Jack a cigarette. Jack takes it and smokes awhile. Silence.
MANAGER: I'm sorry but I have other appointments today.
JACK: Oh yes, I see.
Jack puts out the cigarette and jumps into the "furnace." In an instant he is consumed—nothing more remains.

Scene 15

An empty stage, as it was at the start of the play. William Shakespeare enters. He drags a beer case with empty bottles. Silence. He gazes at the audience for a while.
SHAKESPEARE: People are always
        Being born.
        Bodies are always popping
        Out of bodies.
        Mothers still lick the wounds
        Of their children.
        They follow their steps
        With baited breath;
        The old ones wait at the base of the mountain.
        The young ones approach from all sides
        And run uphill.
        A machine appears on the horizon.
        It consumes the runners
        In a smokeless void
        An early death comes hot on the trail
        Of a careening life.
Shakespeare kneels down and places his ear to the ground, Indian-style.
SHAKESPEARE: I ask for complete quiet.
        Beneath this stage
        I hear the voices
        Of the dead who died too soon.
        The great dead, of course,
        Have all had their say—
        Standing on this stage
        Before they died
        They delivered long monologues.
        Quiet, please.

Here is one—
He didn't say much
He was no literary voice.
Still he's down there—
Who are you, pal?
Silence. Shakespeare directs his words to the stage floor.
SHAKESPEARE: Are you a young commander
Who found his abrupt, yet glorious end
Leading his younger soldiers?
Come on up to the stage.
Silence.
SHAKESPEARE: Are you a singer
Inexperienced in love
Who sang her own swan-song
Wrapped in sorrow?
Come on up to the stage.
Silence.
SHAKESPEARE: Are you a drunkard?
A womanizer?
Have you whored or stuffed your face?
Did you waste your time
With drinking buddies
Doing stupid things?
Did your immoderate life
Bring about your early death?
Come on up to the stage.
Silence.
SHAKESPEARE: Were you deformed?
Really a mess?
When mothers saw you
Did they scream
Did dogs run from you?
Were children traumatized
For life when they saw you?
Did all that disgust
Cause your young death?
Come on up to the stage.
Silence.
SHAKESPEARE: Are you an author?
A poet?

>   Whom the weight of the world,
>   Like a stone about your neck
>   Drove into dangerous waters?
>   Come on up to the stage.

Silence.

SHAKESPEARE: Pal,
>   Did the war eat you up?
>   Flesh and blood
>   And name?
>   Do you lie in an unknown grave
>   Where the flowers foul the air?
>   Come on up to the stage?

Silence.

SHAKESPEARE: Did you die in the street?
>   In the dust and fumes
>   In the fumes and dust?
>   Were you buried with all the pomp
>   A cop could muster?
>   Come on up to the stage.

Silence.

SHAKESPEARE: Whoever you may be—
>   A poor or rich man
>   Handsome or ugly
>   Meaningful or meaningless:
>   Come on up to the stage—
>   This is the place.

Shakespeare places his ear to the ground.

SHAKESPEARE: I ask for quiet
>   And respect—
>   A young corpse speaks.

Silence. Shakespeare places his ear to the ground again. He listens, he stands up, looks at the audience; shrugs his shoulders.

SHAKESPEARE: He says
>   He's just a thing.

Shakespeare kneels again and speaks to the stage floor.

SHAKESPEARE: What kind of thing?

He listens.

SHAKESPEARE: An iron thing?
>   Iron?
>   There are a lot of things made of iron.

222 *The Slackers*

> *He listens. He stands up and again shrugs his shoulders.*

SHAKESPEARE: He used to be a man
               Now he's a thing
               A thing made out of iron.
               That's all we know.

> *Shakespeare speaks—apparently lifelessly—with the audience.*

SHAKESPEARE: Is this man
               Who was a man
               A nail now somewhere in a crossbeam?
               A piece of railroad track
               Lying between two towns?
               A chic lamp, perhaps?
               Hanging over the beds
               Of the rich and famous?
               A fence—barbed wire—
               Between two warring neighbors?
               Forceps? A car door?
               Maybe he's a nameplate
               With a foreign name.
               Or a bridge piling
               In a raging river?
               A rusting gutter
               Or the key to a treasure box?
               Is his eye now a bell
               His guts a chassis?
               Does his heart wait
               In the mill to be processed?
               Who knows?

> *Suddenly, he sobs, then cries out.*

               Who knows
               Who knows
               Who knows!

> *Shakespeare speaks softly again.*

SHAKESPEARE: Why can't I be a thing?
               So many have handled me
               Yet I've been touched by no one.

> *He sings.*

SHAKESPEARE: I was almost something
               Until rescued by my pal.

> *He speaks.*

SHAKESPEARE: I was the empty bottle
Lying beside the dying body
The lamp above the death rattle,
Still burning.
I was the mouth
Bringing news of
The annihilation.

He sings.

SHAKESPEARE: I was almost something, too,
Until rescued by my pal.

He screams.

SHAKESPEARE: Why can't I be like this silver plate
In my skull!?
Cold and metallic and...

He takes one bottle after the other from the case of beer and smashes it on his head. He laughs.

SHAKESPEARE: Well.
I'm all right, Jack
How 'bout you?

END

AFTERWORD

I first met Peter Turrini in 1978 at the Café Grillparzer in Vienna. We met to discuss the possible translation of his first play, *rozznjogd*, (1967/71), a difficult work in the tradition of Peter Handke's *Publikumsbeschimpfung*, which Turrini had written in strong Austrian dialect. As we sat under the low light of the Grillparzer's sixty-watt bulbs our discussion soon moved beyond the original reason for our meeting. We touched on a number of issues that were then, at the beginning of Turrini's rise in stature as a playwright, quite important to him.

Even then, Turrini regarded himself as somewhat of a "prisoner" of his biography. His writing sought to express this idea; it still does. Growing up in the small Carinthian town of Maria Saal, Turrini had an uneasy relationship with his surroundings: the people and traditions of southern Austria. As the son of an Italian immigrant, he never seemed to feel the warmth of the cozy mantel of *Heimat*, which is so important in those distant, non-Viennese corners of the Austrian Republic. The estrangement from a close provincial security has allowed him to view his country with an increasingly critical eye. Critical, and yet, not unloving.

Turrini calls himself, ironically, a *Heimatdichter*. This is a term difficult to render into English, for it carries with it more than the suggestion that such a writer uses as his theme the pathos of folksy drama. Turrini uses the term in a serious attempt to confront his audience with the issues of his plays, and their context within the idea of *Heimat*. Any modern Austrian writer must, to some extent, confront the stereotype of his own Austrianness. For, if "Austria" has any meaning to a general audience of the twentieth century, that meaning has been shaped largely by the Austria of "The Sound of Music" or the Lippizaner or of a *verkitscht* Mozart and Strauss. Turrini uses our awareness of these symbols to moves his audience away from the idea of "happy" Austria, toward the recognition that Austria, like other industrialized nations, rests uneasily between a past of dubious traditions and a future of precarious humanity. The four plays presented here all have this, ultimately, as their theme.

By turning Beaumarchais (and Mozart!) on his head, by

emphasizing the oppressive nature of the Duke's relationship with Figaro and Susanne, Turrini strips the play of its veneer of cuteness and confronts us with the reality of twentieth-century politics through the images of eighteenth-century aristocratic brutality. This helps to explain the quotation from Beaumarchais that introduces *A Crazy Day* (1972). Turrini emphasizes a key element of Beaumarchais' play that has been overlooked in our awe of Mozart.

The dark vision of *A Crazy Day* has been balanced somewhat by *Joseph and Mary* (1980). Here Turrini has chosen to retell the Christmas story in a way that seeks to reestablish his audience's relationship with the original Christmas story. Joseph and Mary are demythologized in the oddest of ways. Their manger is the darkness of a modern department store; their prayers are the memories of minor lives passed among great images of greed and mercantile inhumanity. The birth that comes to pass on that Christmas night is more a re-birth, an awakening of sorts. The play does not end apocalyptically, but rather hopefully—false illusions are cast aside; Joseph and Mary recognize the true nature of their existence, both present and past. It is a gentle play of revelation.

Revelatory, yet ungentle, is Turrini's next work, *A Social Engagement* (1981), which was a social scandal when it first hit the theater. Many notables of Viennese society thought to have recognized themselves portrayed in the play and took great offense. The play has a broader significance, however, than merely as a mirror to a contemporary version of a stereotypical jaded and decadent Viennese society. Turrini continues the theme of *Heimat*; he continues to confront his audience with the reality of their just or unjust aspirations. The Duke, Figaro, and Susanne of *A Crazy Day* emerge from their costumes to assume modern form. Turrini continues the themes of his previous works, laying bare the nature of relationships, once perceived as cozy, which are, in truth, oppressive and the undoing of our humanity. What had been the cruelty of ducal privilege, becomes the tyranny of consumerism or classism or sexism. That this work ends with a death on stage (suicide!) points to the angry nature of Turrini's political dramaturgy.

One of Turrini's most recent plays, *The Slackers* (1989), is perhaps the most complex of the four presented in this volume.

There is a bit of all the previous works in this one play. Revolutionary activism, social criticism, and lyrical surrealism combine here to form a bitter articulation of the human condition pressed against the wall of a consumer-oriented capitalism. The death of the Duke in *A Crazy Day* suggests revolution as an antidote to social injustice. Jack's death here has no such revolutionary echo. Heiner's suicide in *A Social Engagement* leaves the others with the challenge of interpreting the death, for the suicide can be an end or beginning—it is an open challenge. Jack's death leaves us with no such challenge, for it is the almost inevitable result of a compassionless society. Condemned to death, without the possibility of salvation, Jack leaps into the blast furnace that, earlier, had defined his existence. Joseph and Mary struggle through the night with their own impossible lives; by daybreak, a new understanding sets in. Any transcendent quality of Jack's struggle is extinguished by the heat of the blast furnace. Even the poet Shakespeare gives us no direction, no hope for higher meaning. The play's conclusion, darkest of all, leaves us with only the uneasy echo of Shakespeare's question, posed to a smug and self-satisfied modern theater audience—"I'm all right, Jack; how 'bout you?" This is Turrini's most direct assault upon his audience since the play, *rozznjogd*, where actors portraying hunters open fire on the audience, identifying them as so many "rats" loose in a trash dump.

A word about the translations is in order. The ideal behind this English version of Turrini is a simple one: to present Turrini's plays in English in a form that seeks to reproduce the energetic level of the original German. This poses the usual translation problems, of course. The translation is not a word-for-word literal translation. What I have tried to do is give the reader (or audience) a sense of the original German by way of "original" English. That will explain minor deviations in detail, especially where verse or meter or cultural icons are concerned.

Still, the plays are wholly Turrini; I have not presumed to change that in any way. Peter Turrini is a singularly important voice on the German language stage. Up until now no translations of his works (besides brief bits of poetry) have been available to an English-speaking audience. The goal of this volume is to bring Turrini to that audience in as lively and engaging a manner as a

German-speaking audience encounters him. Retaining the vigor of language was of great importance to Turrini as we discussed our first project together in the Café Grillparzer so many years ago; it remains my primary objective in the translation of four important works of this Austrian playwright. Peter Turrini will continue to be a force to reckon with on the European stage for years to come; it is hoped that, through this translation, English-speaking audiences can understand why.

—Richard S. Dixon

STUDIES IN AUSTRIAN LITERATURE, CULTURE, AND THOUGHT

*Major Figures of
Modern Austrian Literature*
Edited by
Donald G. Daviau

*Major Figures of
Turn-of-the-Century
Austrian Literature*
Edited by Donald G. Daviau

*Austrian Writers and the
Anschluss: Understanding the
Past—Overcoming the Past*
Edited by Donald G. Daviau

*Introducing Austria
A Short History*
By Lonnie Johnson

*Austrian Foreign Policy
Yearbook*
Report of the Austrian Federal
Ministry for Foreign Affairs
for the Year 1990

*The Verbal and Visual Art of
Alfred Kubin*
By Phillip H. Rhein

Arthur Schnitzler and Politics
By Adrian Clive Roberts

*Austria in the Thirties
Culture and Politics*
Edited by Kenneth Segar
and John Warren

*Stefan Zweig:
An International Bibliography*
By Randolf J. Klawiter

*"What People Call Pessimism":
Sigmund Freud, Arthur Schnitzler
and Nineteenth-Century
Controversy at the University
of Vienna Medical School*
By Mark Luprecht

*Quietude and Quest
Protagonists and Antagonists in
the Theater, on and off Stage
As seen through the Eyes of
Leon Askin*
Leon Askin and C. Melvin Davidson

*Coexistent Contradictions
Joseph Roth in Retrospect*
Edited by
Helen Chambers

*Kafka and Language
In the Stream of
Thoughts and Life*
By G. von Natzmer Cooper

ARIADNE PRESS

TRANSLATION SERIES:

February Shadows
By Elisabeth Reichart
Translated by Donna L. Hofmeister
Afterword by Christa Wolf

Night Over Vienna
By Lili Körber
Translated by Viktoria Hertling
and Kay M. Stone. Commentary
by Viktoria Hertling

The Cool Million
By Erich Wolfgang Skwara
Translated by Harvey I. Dunkle
Preface by Martin Walser
Afterword by Richard Exner

Buried in the Sands of Time
Poetry by Janko Ferk
English/German/Slovenian
English Translation
by Herbert Kuhner

Puntigam or The Art of Forgetting
By Gerald Szyszkowitz
Translated by Adrian Del Caro
Preface by Simon Wiesenthal
Afterword by Jürgen Koppensteiner

Negatives of My Father
By Peter Henisch
Translated and with an Afterword
by Anne C. Ulmer

On the Other Side
By Gerald Szyszkowitz
Translated by Todd C. Hanlin
Afterword by Jürgen Koppensteiner

*I Want to Speak
The Tragedy and Banality
of Survival in
Terezin and Auschwitz*
By Margareta Glas-Larsson
Edited and with a Commentary
by Gerhard Botz
Translated by Lowell A. Bangerter

The Works of Solitude
By György Sebestyén
Translated and with an
Afterword by
Michael Mitchell

Remembering Gardens
By Kurt Klinger
Translated by Harvey I. Dunkle

Deserter
By Anton Fuchs
Translated and with an Afterword
by Todd C. Hanlin

From Here to There
By Peter Rosei
Translated and with an Afterword
by Kathleen Thorpe

The Angel of the West Window
By Gustav Meyrink
Translated by Michael Mitchell

*Relationships
An Anthology of Contemporary
Austrian Literature*
Selected and with an Introduction
by Adolf Opel